Generative AI for Marketing

Generative AI for Marketing

Malay A. Upadhyay

BEP

BUSINESS EXPERT PRESS

Leader in applied, concise business books

Generative AI for Marketing

Cover image created with Microsoft Copilot, designed by
Malay A. Upadhyay and Pooja Chitnis, and formatted by Michelle Li

Interior design by Exeter Premedia Services Private Ltd., Chennai, India

First published in 2024 by
Business Expert Press, LLC
222 East 46th Street, New York, NY 10017
www.businessexpertpress.com

ISBN-13: 978-1-63742-716-3 (paperback)
ISBN-13: 978-1-63742-717-0 (e-book)

Business Expert Press Marketing Collection

First edition: 2024

10 9 8 7 6 5 4 3 2 1

To those who love a miracle from Santa Claus on Christmas
as much as they love good deals on Boxing Day…
and choose to offer both.

Description

Every few generations, a technoeconomic revolution topples the status quo of how work is done, creating an opportunity for new leaders to emerge. *Generative AI for Marketing* is meant to position the current and future marketers to become those leaders and lead their organizations in the AI era.

To succeed in leveraging AI, organizations must look beyond practices that were established before the AI era. This book elucidates the evolving role and needs of Generative AI in marketing, providing a blueprint for businesses to thrive in an ever-evolving business landscape by achieving the agility and adaptability needed to sustain growth with AI.

Tailored for marketers and business students alike, readers will gain a commanding set of tools to master the trifecta of foundational AI knowledge, its applications in Marketing, and the knowhow to automate growth without increasing costs.

Contents

Testimonials

"*In this groundbreaking book, Malay Upadhyay demystifies AI for marketing professionals while introducing a revolutionary functional structure for organizations looking to embrace the future. By shifting traditional functions into project areas and reimagining marketing organizations around three core functions—Content Creation, Automation, and Insights Generation—this insightful guide embodies the principles of frugal innovation. It enables companies to navigate the dynamic landscape of AI, fostering agility and strategic alignment, and enabling innovation that is faster, better and cheaper. A must-read for anyone seeking to harness the full potential of generative AI in marketing and stay ahead in this rapidly evolving field.*"—**Jaideep Prabhu, professor of marketing and Nehru professor of Indian business at the University of Cambridge's Judge Business School**

"*In these early days of AI most books focus solely on the 'how to.' By contrast, Malay looks at the evolution of marketing to predict where it is going and the evolution of AI to see the next logical steps in its evolution. He then blends those analyses to give readers a glimpse of how AI will be applied to marketing in the future. The result is a power user's guide. Whether the predictions prove true or not, the issues and questions he discusses are ones that every marketer should be considering.*"—**Kenneth B. Wong, advisory board member of the Level5 Strategy Group and the distinguished professor of marketing and business strategy at Queen's University's Smith School of Business**

"*AI has become an integral facet of our daily existence, marketing and sales leaders are quickly revolutionizing how they engage with customers with Generative AI. This book looks at the historical perspective of technology, marketing and sales to shape the future of revenue-driven functions. It also highlights the critical impact of AI on our socio-cultural milieu, underscoring the imperative for Responsible AI and Governance. It's a great read for anyone in sales and marketing to take a deeper look into how AI is recalibrating our way of operating, reexamining our relationships with customers—and harnessing AI ethically for a better world."*—**Linh C. Ho, serial tech startup adviser and investor, and a board director at Cascade PBS**

"As marketers embrace the AI evolution, they're rapidly researching, generating, distributing, and optimizing multimedia content at unprecedented rates, all while maintaining high editorial standards. This book empowers creatives to unlock GenAI-enabled product potential through team optimization and process automation."—**Bryan Larson, VP strategy, Vendasta**

"When it comes to trends in how business and technology intersect, Malay is among the best there is. AI has been his focus and passion for many years, so Malay goes beyond the Chat-GPT hype to provide rich analysis and tangible takeaways. Whether Malay's speaking on a panel, conducting a masterclass, writing a book, or putting theory into practice at work, he always conveys information with a unique clarity and depth."—**Rob Manne, founder at Inflectiv and former VP at Edelman and Interbrand**

Foreword

My interest in AI originated from Isaac Asimov's robot stories, eventually driving me to pursue a PhD in the field. Currently chief AI officer at Scotiabank, my journey afforded me a firsthand view of the transformative impact of AI over the years. Beyond a mere academic pursuit, AI has evolved into a dynamic force molding the essence of various industries. Today, I believe that the arrival of generative AI marks a turning point in the world of marketing.

Malay and I nurtured a camaraderie in our leadership roles at SalesChoice—an AI-driven company specializing in sales enablement. Throughout our journey, we engaged in spirited debates on the profound impact of AI on the world—more often than not around a nice dinner. Some of these conversations shaped Malay's other books on AI and marketing. One of the many points of agreement between us is the recognition that, within the ever-evolving landscape of marketing, change is the only constant. The dynamics of the profession are in perpetual flux, demanding marketers to continuously adapt, innovate, and redefine strategies in response to the shifting tides.

Enter generative AI—the revolutionary force poised to redefine marketing as we know it. The advent of GenAI marks a pivotal moment, promising capabilities that extend beyond the boundaries of conventional marketing strategies. It's not merely a tool; it's a catalyst for innovation, offering the potential to unlock new dimensions in our quest for effective and impactful marketing.

However, the integration of generative AI is not a simple substitution of people with technology. It's a nuanced relationship where the tool complements human expertise, offering possibilities that transcend individual capacities. This book aims to dispel the notion of GenAI as a replacement and, instead, positions it as a powerful collaborator in the hands of skilled marketers.

To that effect, this book illuminates the process of positioning organizations to enable generative AI effectively. For marketing managers and practitioners, it provides a roadmap for leveraging GenAI for marketing success. The book serves as a guide through the complexities, offering insights on how to make the best of GenAI in a manner that is both productive and aligned with legal and ethical considerations.

In the pages that follow, prepare to embark on a journey that transcends conventional marketing wisdom. As we stand at the intersection of change and innovation, may this book be your compass, guiding you through the complexities and possibilities that generative AI introduces to the world of marketing.

—Dr. Yannick Lallement

Preface

Generative AI is one of the most ground-breaking innovations of our generation. It has brought artificial intelligence to our very doorstep and finally compelled us to adopt it as direct and conscious users. In doing so, it may be on course to join a select and royal list of ageless innovations that include the likes of personal computers—and if one may stretch it—penicillin, internal combustion engines, and the wheel.

Is generative AI really that important? And what makes it so? Innovations take time to become the fundamental socioeconomic drivers of an age. It is the one most adaptable to changing social needs that eventually transcends time. Computers existed as a complex mysterious entity for decades before Microsoft brought it into our homes in the form of personal computers. That was when it crossed the chasm and the rest is history. AI is at a similar stage. In its 2020 Jobs report, the World Economic Forum predicted that AI will displace 85 million jobs and create 97 million others The displacement and creation don't occur simultaneously in their entirety and often harbor an unsettled transition period. We may not have known the exact mechanism of these changes, but it seems increasingly likely that we do now.

As we will see in this book, there is a reason why generative AI has the potential to disrupt and evolve work across all management functions—one built on years of iterative advances and morphing market demand. Consequently, the way organizations structure their functions must change as well. One area has been experiencing the generative AI disruption more significantly than the rest do. After all, the art of *generating* imagery, voice, video, text, and other content forms to attract and capture the audience's attention has long been the domain of a marketer. There is, however, more to it than meets the eye.

Gone are the days when marketing implied promotions and advertisements alone. Today, it reflects the entire growth agenda, acting as a common vein running through an organization—from its products to its value proposition, from its market presence to sales cycles, and from postsale services to its revenue and cost analytics. So, vibrations in this function tend to propagate through the entire organization.

This book will focus on how marketing must be restructured along functions and projects and how organizational growth can leverage generative AI tools like ChatGPT, the crowning jewel of this technology's ongoing surge. We will begin by looking at the past. Why is that? It is because most tools we know today may not stand the test of time. So, instead of bulking up on our knowledge of a few tools, it is more important to stay on top of how the technologies and our dependencies are evolving, why, and how to prepare for it. Only by understanding the trajectory of past changes can we reliably uncover that and stay prepared for what the future brings.

Part 1 of this book will trace the evolution of marketing to look at where it fits in an evolving organizational model, what forces are straining organizations today, and why traditional silos within marketing may not be effective in a data and insight-driven age. Truly effective predictive insights are about finding the right patterns in a timely manner. For instance, customer-related data from every touchpoint within and outside the organization must be assembled to ensure that customer acquisition or retention strategies not only see a positive Return on Investment (ROI) but are also sustainable.

Speaking of sustainability, cost control would require a lot of strategic execution to be automated, not so much to replace workers but to augment their productivity manifold. That in turn will bring us to Part 2 of the book, which will slice through the noise to transude the essence of AI. What is it, what makes it an inevitable force, and how did we get to the birth of generative AI? Most importantly, what are some of the best practices to follow in AI journeys? One cannot master a force without understanding it first.

Part 3 will look at the new functional and project-based structure that can optimally drive AI-driven marketing organizations. It will cover prompting techniques, content creation, process automation, and insight generation—the latter three imagined as three functions that can supply resources and ensure informed decision making and alignment across the many project areas. These areas are what have traditionally been siloed marketing domains impeding the use of AI. Part 3 will explain how agility to course correct in the face of changing organizational and market realities, real-time information exchange, and cross-functional alignment are key to maximizing the returns from AI.

Finally, in Part 4, having grasped the technologies and organizational changes, we will now see what future the patterns point to. That is, after all, the principle of pattern recognition that all AI is built on. We will conclude our journey with a summary for easy reference, to contextualize this evolutionary techno-economic cycle we find ourselves in.

This book is a treasure trove packed with unique and immediately usable assets to empower the readers with everything they need to know, quickly. On one hand, they will journey through the concepts of artificial intelligence, generative AI, large language models, and ChatGPT; understand its origins, risks, and future; and gain frameworks and methodologies simplifying these seemingly complex topics for day-to-day use at work. On the other hand, they will learn to look at marketing like never before, from the combined lens of both a customer and the organization, thereby appreciating the facets of generative AI initiatives to use and why.

With every revolutionary breakthrough comes an opportunity for people to define their careers. It was true for the gold rush of 1849 as much as it was for the Internet boom of the 1990s. What people need in such times is to act quickly and a tool to act with. This book offers the latter for marketers and entrepreneurs who wish to do the former. By the end of their journey, the readers may well have crossed a chasm of their own—from one of the 85 million to be potentially displaced by AI to one of the 97 million ready for the future.

Acknowledgments

A book owes its life to many stakeholders. The author may give it a shape, and the publisher's production team and reviewers may polish it, but it's the readers who give it meaning and relevance. Without all three, a gemstone is but a rock. And yet, the list of contributors doesn't stop here. A book's content—a translation of the author's thought—owes its genesis and evolution to those who surround and influence him every day. This acknowledgment goes to all.

I would like to begin, as always, by thanking my guru, Sree Sai. Given the unexpected upheaval that coincided with writing this book, to have finished the manuscript in time and in the form that you now see is nothing short of a miracle. That grace and fortitude is a gift that demands faith. And much like the advanced concepts of AI discussed in this book, unflinching faith has certain prerequisites of its own: a deeply personal and spiritual guide is one of them. A guru is one of its most potent forms.

As important as a spiritual guide is, so is the supportive rock in one's life. In sharing the ups and downs with me and bearing with the commitment this book took, my partner, Pooja, deserves every bit of my immense gratitude. Thank you for the little details you bring to my day that make such endeavors possible.

Next, I would like to thank my publisher, Business Expert Press, and all involved in bringing this book to market. Nigel Wyatt and Scott Isenberg for their receptivity to the initial book idea; Naresh Malhotra, Emeritus Professor of Marketing at the Georgia Institute of Technology for his glowing support of this project; Charlene Kronstedt in the production and marketing team; the editing team at Exeter, and everyone else involved in the publication is as vital as the cogs that support any production line. The book would not have been a reality without you. Thank you.

My gratitude also goes out to my past publisher, BPB Publications, who brought the original AI Management series of three books to life. These books covered the basics of AI and marketing and paved the way for this one that not only brings the two fields together but reimagines the management approaches to support the union.

Yannick Lallement, chief AI officer at Scotiabank, is one of the humblest representations of genius that I have ever come across—the kind of equanimity and surety one instantly begins to aspire toward. If his introductory contribution to this book is a privilege, his friendship and the laughs we periodically share are an even greater one I'm fortunate to have.

Jaideep Prabhu, professor of marketing and Nehru professor of Indian business at the University of Cambridge's Judge Business School; Kenneth B. Wong, advisory board member of the Level5 Strategy Group and the distinguished professor of marketing and business strategy at Queen's University's Smith School of Business; Linh C. Ho, a serial tech startup adviser and investor, and a board director at Cascade PBS; Bryan Larson, VP strategy, Vendasta; and Rob Manne, founder at Inflectiv and former VP at Edelman and Interbrand; have been some of the prominent industry voices in the field. I'm always honored to hear their perspectives. Their words of endorsement embellish this book as beautifully as any alchemy would.

Finally, I would like to acknowledge Genevieve Bonin, managing director and partner at the Boston Consulting Group, for introducing me to their concept of generative leadership. I must also mention Bocconi University for having built my foundations in marketing so sturdily all those years ago, and Archit Chitnis, whose mandate as a head of product and digital payments includes data and AI solutions thinking. It was our casual brainstorming one summer evening on the drivers of success and failures with AI that sowed the seeds of some of the structural ideas that I now share with you.

PART 1

The Changing Landscape of Marketing

Study the past, if you would divine the future.

—Confucius

Generative AI (Artificial Intelligence) for marketing refers to enabling the many subfunctions of the marketing domain with this new technology. If one meets a marketer today, odds are that individual would be highly specialized in one area of this domain. As such, content marketers may struggle with product strategy, while account-based marketers may struggle with channel marketing.

When generative AI is used well, it can lead to new or augmented product offerings and cost-reduction automation, among other things. But to use it well for the organization, marketers must understand how, when and where to use it—not to mention what it really is and how it works. How can we achieve that if marketers remain in silos? And how can they restructure themselves without understanding the role that marketing is supposed to play in AI-enabled organizations?

Organizational structures are currently in a transitionary period dictated not only by the changing market demand but also by the very nature of AI. As we will see in Part 2, AI's strength is in recognizing patterns. Hidden patterns—especially those we are blind to—are revealed more accurately when the quality and volume of data increases. That is why generative AI requires functional collaboration, to accomplish which we must map the stakeholders, processes, and even the context around any planning and execution.

So, before we talk about how an organization can generate growth from generative AI tools or models, let's understand the shifting realities that marketers have to tackle, and how we can navigate functional complexities to enable that growth.

Over the next two chapters, we will discover how marketing within organizations is taking shape to be driven by data and insights, why that is so, and how resources from within and beyond the function can be involved in realizing its many objectives. The first chapter will trace the steps of history to place prevalent operating models in context, followed by a look at the realities that organizations today operate in. The second chapter will then extend it to how marketing can operate effectively in these new realities.

CHAPTER 1

Evolution of the Marketing Organization

Entrée

We live in a world of cause and effect. To leverage generative AI in marketing, we must first remove the organizational barriers that limit returns from AI initiatives. For those barriers to surface, we need to understand the structures and processes they reside in, and how and why they came to be the way they are. So, in this chapter, we will trace the evolution of marketing, the forces that drove it to reach a state that now impedes AI, and how it is changing today. We will also touch upon the principal objective that has governed all this change—one that is now incentivizing us to use generative AI—achieving brand resonance.

Marketing took birth to help organizations sell better. That purpose has not changed, but the approach has—from creating points of differentiation to enabling new channels of purchase. It has always been a supply-and-demand game. Suppliers attempt to scoop a slice of the demand (if not the whole pie), grow it to make room for themselves, or simply create more. All three routes deal with influencing the customer. Did we know we needed a phone, camera, and music player in one device until Apple released the iPhone?

A marketer's job has always been to deliver on that strategic goal of customer influence, whether it's to defeat the competition or create more room for everyone. It may involve psychological manipulation—where increased value is only perceived, not necessarily real—or actual value delivered better than the competitors can. Both require understanding the customer's viewpoint and experience perfectly. Step into the shoes of the customer, as they say.

Understanding something as abstract or subjective as customer behavior is where humans need intelligent augmentation, not because we are not capable of doing so but because we may not be able to do it comprehensively and fast enough. Time is always our greatest resource and impediment, as it directly impacts the cost and competitiveness of any company. Increased productivity in a given timeframe, therefore, increases a company's odds of success. That, in a nutshell, is what AI is meant for.

Productivity can have different meanings and be measured differently in different circumstances. It depends on the team measuring productivity and the business need it is trying to fulfill. Accordingly, it could imply the number of social media posts generated per resource hour, the number of engagements per post, the number of customer conversions per engagement, or—coming back full circle—the revenue generated per resource hour.

Changing circumstances alter the business needs and, by extension, the metrics. The organizational circumstances have changed quite a bit over the decades, and even more so over the recent pandemic years, aided by the evolution continuum of how business is done globally. Anticipating these changes is important because, as Part 2 of this book will show, errors in what is being measured are a common cause of failed investments in AI. Even 99 percent accurate AI models can be hiding millions of dollars in lost revenues! Looking at parameters that did not accurately reflect the changing market is what hid the growing threat under high ongoing sales for the American video retail store chain, Blockbuster, and eventually led to its demise.

Metrics are not the only cause of failures in AI investments, of course. An organization's readiness to use and support AI is another major factor. The traditional structures were not built with the requirements of this technology in mind; they were built to address a different set of challenges. So, to understand how marketing organizations should set themselves up to optimally leverage generative AI, let us make sense of why they are currently structured the way they are and why that creates friction in leveraging AI.

The Evolutionary Journey of Marketing

Let's rewind the clock back over a hundred years as companies of the early Industrial Ages had moved on from systems of trade and barter, thanks to new machinery, and mass production first took hold. Over the first few decades in the late 19th and early 20th centuries, scattered mass-producing companies enjoyed an era of market demand outpacing supply. Revenue generation was straightforward as long as a product could be made reasonably available and accessible for purchase. Who doesn't remember Henry Ford's famous line: Any customer can have a car painted any color that he wants so long as it is black. Product differentiation seemed to be missing from the agenda.

Functional areas first took shape when mass production began to dictate more sophisticated management to handle the volumes. Take the structure at the time of Henry Ford, for example, where accountabilities were distributed by functions, followed by subfunctions and so on. Sales, purchasing, service, and accounting reported to one financial leader under Mr. Ford, who also had research, legal, and production under him. The latter branched into several subareas over two or three levels, all the way down to the respective parts of the car being produced.

It wasn't until the postwar era of rebuilding and growing societies—and an exploding population in times of peace—that marketing was first born. Companies now faced with competition on a local or global level realized that establishing differentiation in their offerings was key to customer acquisition. Brand recognition and credibility became important to build customer loyalty. The tool of choice was to embed a positive association in the customer's memory—Christmas, game nights, romantic dates, and social stature were a few of the most common ones. The first age of marketing began with an eye on building resonance.

Brand resonance often fades in the face of brand loyalty—an elusive goal most marketers try to achieve. Resonance, however, is far more resilient and crucial to sustain a brand's existence and growth. Loyalties can change due to a host of factors—affordability, fad, convenience, and temporal irrelevance, to name a few. Resonance is sticky because it clings to a customer's self-identity. That's something deeply personal, fiercely defended, and relatively everlasting.

Choosing the right approach early to build resonance is crucial because once resonant, a brand may cease to exist without it. Resonance typically requires a brand to consistently and convincingly meet one of the VAMP criteria for its target audience. It constitutes values (or beliefs), aspirations (or inherent desires), memory (or nostalgia), or personality (or identity) that a customer carries. The nature of its offering typically limits a company to one or two of these conditions that it can reliably cater to. They can be notoriously difficult to gauge and achieve, making the organizations that command resonance across any of these four conditions a rarity. Yet, the subjectivity of the factors that have traditionally made resonance evasive can now be addressed with generative AI, as we will see in this book.

In the early era, resonance was attempted by a few companies and with unique entities that customers loved. There was room for everyone, in a way, to find a consumer love to associate with. As competition grew, markets opened globally, and supply began to keep pace with demand, resonant entities began to thin out. After all, if more than one perfume brand promised a successful date night, it was difficult for a consumer to trust or choose just one.

In a room with several men standing with a bouquet of roses, all vying for the attention of one person, looking good was not enough to stand out. It now became important to try and build a personal rapport with the target. As resonance became harder to achieve through associations and meaning alone, marketing initiated its attempt at forging relationships, ideally long-term. That involved diversifying the product to find niches and to evolve with changing consumer tastes. The long game came into focus, and customer retention grew to be just as important as customer acquisition. The customer success function branched out from marketing.

So, we had sales as the original child, which gave birth to marketing. The latter focused on advertising to drive sales. Brand building was key but concerned itself more with the implied message and the choice of association. Content creation remained somewhat pedestrian. As the market became crowded, we witnessed the arrival of product marketing to cater to niches, channel marketing to ensure their visibility and easy retail access for customers, and customer success to sustain them. The organization was thus far stratified functionally. And then came the Internet.

Diversification of products had an interesting influence on the next era as room for new products began to thin out, offshoring made production cheaper, and the service industry grew. Meanwhile, as the digital era took hold, newer companies began to organize themselves divisionally. This requirement was primarily influenced by the sheer range of product and service offerings that companies could now take to market. Think about Amazon today and its divisional setup around subscriptions (Prime), Amazon Web Services, third-party seller services, and so on. Globalization also meant territorial divisions based on distinct geographic regions. Coupled with the divisions around functions and offerings, it resulted in a matrix structure where organizations were structured along multiple parameters.

The digital era also cast an obvious trance on marketing as social media marketers, e-mail marketers, digital advertisers, SEO experts, and e-commerce specialists arrived, distinguishing themselves from the offline marketing focus of events and retail. Given the matrix organizational structures, diverse customer profiles across different geographies and distinctly different products aimed at different buyers, marketing found itself stretched and meshed across product and service offerings, geographies, and subfunctions.

If that feels complex, it was all about to receive an added push. Demand and supply had reached a point where carving a blue ocean had become ever more crucial to survive and grow. A blue ocean is a niche within an industry with limited or no competition where a brand can enjoy a first-mover advantage. Think about the soft drinks industry. When soda, fruit juice, iced tea, and bottled water seemed to have captured every possible demand for this industry, it was believed that there was no room for a new product category. Yet, energy drinks and flavored water took the market by storm, propelling Red Bull and Gatorade to heights that had been reserved for the likes of Coca-Cola.

Finding a blue ocean by-product was not feasible in every industry. In most cases, a niche was found with existing products attuned to specific customer segments. Successful companies were identifying and addressing niche consumer groups that had a need unmet by available offerings in the market. That necessitated more acute market research and customer insights. Data was now beginning to monetize itself.

The limited approach to marketing caused an interesting anomaly in a marketer's career. Marketing came to imply a specific aspect of this massively broad domain based on which industry or growth stage one worked in. Most marketers found themselves working in limited areas of marketing, either due to the company's limited appetite or its siloed structures. For instance, smaller companies—that are typically faced with enabling growth amidst resource crunch—had to prioritize product development and sales.

While marketing found itself tucked once again under sales in smaller companies, larger and fast-growing companies—those with ample resources but a need for aggressive competitive advantage—invested in varied forms of marketing, with a separate team for each area. Even in industries like fast-moving consumer goods (FMCG), which banked on marketing for revenue generation, distinct subfunctions had to be set up due to the sheer breadth and scale of the tasks involved. After all, one resource would find it tough to juggle content creation, market research, and retail channel enablement at the scale needed. Gradually, the silos became the norm.

Market fragmentation due to ever-diversifying consumer tastes had begun to strain the marketer's world. As companies tried to find and cater to niche customer segments, their advertisers had no choice but to rely on the media providers' claims on which advertising channel was more efficient for a particular customer niche. While the dollars flowed out under such assumptions over the first decade of the new millennium, many of these differentiating claims turned out to be largely inconsequential, as revealed by a 2010 study.[1]

Market competition continued increasing in the second decade of the 21st century, aided by the postrecession boom in demand and the age of venture capitalists and start-ups. It intensified the need to produce offerings and adapt to changing market dynamics even more quickly. When complexity in structures clashed with the need for agility, it gave rise to a new structural norm of a relatively flat hierarchy.

It began with start-ups, where the priority was to generate and bring value to the market. Everything else—from office spaces to processes was purposefully made minimalistic to avoid investing limited resources in operational areas that did not directly influence revenue generation. Marketers were still allocated to specific subtasks, but marketing as a functional area was starting to become more fluid, its boundaries beginning to smudge in a company's revenue growth agenda. And that brings us to the present era.

These structures—complex or minimalist—were designed to prioritize certain management objectives over allowing a seamless flow of information and insights. The strain they feel today is due to a shift in those objectives where timely insights and resource optimization are starting to take priority for an organization's very survival. To mull over how the organizations should shape up to optimize AI usage for these new objectives, let us venture a little deeper into these ongoing shifts.

The Ongoing Organizational Shift

All through its evolutionary journey, Marketing has undergone alterations due to forces both external to an organization and ones within it. That remains true today as well, as evident in the external and internal perspectives discussed later. A leader understands the value of mapping these shifts and keeping in touch with them. As a 1992 study on market fragmentation states: "if the CEO fails to recognize these macro-trends, it could mean corporate death. On the other hand, the CEO that does detect a macro-change early in its evolution and constructs a strategy to capitalize on it can reap substantial rewards."[2]

Trends, though, can be found both externally and internally. Let us look at a few influencing organizations.

The External Shift

We briefly spoke about the demand and supply equation and traced how it has shifted over the last century. Overcrowding of the market has also put increased cost pressures on practically every company—either to survive or to sustain growth. At the same time, in an age of behemoth institutional investors riding on the back of an ever-growing population of individual investors globally, pressures to increase earnings remain just as high. Both have had serious consequences.

Shareholders can be quite unforgiving of even the slightest indications of reduced returns, thanks to their ability to quickly sell their shares in one firm and reinvest the capital in another. Take the pharmaceutical firm, Moderna, Inc., which gave us lifesaving Covid-19 vaccines. The company's share price rose over 2,000 percent from early 2020 to Fall 2021. Yet, at one point almost 75 percent of those gains were gone only two years later as investors (many of whose lives the Moderna vaccine had likely saved) began to wonder whether the company could produce another blockbuster drug.

At an institutional level, companies have a very low margin of error to avoid negatively impacting their share price. This, in fact, is one of the primary reasons why they have been so resistant to investing in long-term sustainable solutions and business models, regardless of its impact on the society and planet. It's difficult for a company to sacrifice short-term growth for the benefit of people and planet if the consequent share-holder response can threaten its competitive survival and, eventually, jobs of those very people.

Then, there are the other macroeconomic factors, chief among them the strained nature of our supply chains. Bottlenecks and capacity lim-itations lead to increased cost of resources, worsened by geopolitical rifts. Meanwhile, the earnings pressure mandates improving the cash flow, which invariably brings us back to cost reduction, directly or indirectly influencing jobs again—whether within the company or at any of its vendors.

Why the focus on jobs? Because in an age of automation, only those existing jobs are likely to survive that can truly aid the shifting needs of a company. The others will likely be entirely new jobs that did not exist before. And the transition from the erasure of jobs to the creation of new ones is not always quick. It takes time, and the interlude in between often takes the form of a recession. A recent International Monetary Fund (IMF) analysis estimates that AI is likely to worsen inequality and impact 40 percent of all jobs, most of which would be in advanced economies.[3]

So, a marketer's prerogative is to avoid living in a silo, unaware of oncoming automation that a company may be compelled to adopt in order to tackle the cost and earnings pressures. Such dramatic shifts are often produced by episodes like the pandemic that serve as a generational shock to the system. They expose the superfluous elements of an economic system or introduce more efficient alternatives to running the economy.

When the pandemic hit, most employees were forced to work from home. The remote work culture was only partially reversed once the pandemic was over. Through these years, it built an appetite to experience and adopt automation of work where there used to be resistance to the idea before. This is what made organizations more primed and ready to take the leap when generative AI hit the market.

Prepandemic, most executives were either thinking of experimenting with AI or unsure about its effectiveness in the short term. Fast forward a few years, and the conversation had shifted from whether to use AI to how to use it best. For individual employees, meanwhile, AI went from being some shiny new toy to one worthy of more thought. We saw a similar trend with personal computers. Adoption of any technology or skill among employees is always facilitated and hastened by their employers.

Before a company gets to upskilling its people, the first step that it is likely to encounter on its AI journey is the need to organize itself for better data and processes. That brings us to the internal shifts.

The Internal Shift

Faced with hybrid or remote work, data and processes have either already shifted to the cloud or doing so at an increasing pace today. For a marketer, that means an increase in ease of access to insights, ability to take real-time action, and leadership expectation that they do so. One of the biggest shifts has been the growing prevalence of contactless execution—whether in taking payments, answering queries, or executing paperwork.

We spoke about productivity measures earlier. Consider a creative content artist trying to optimize ad copies. How would she leverage and measure a reinforcement learning system that can run multiple versions of an online advertisement and identify the best one in real time based on the volume and nature of ongoing audience engagement with each advertisement? It may sound complex, but understanding how such a system works can certainly differentiate this artist from her peers.

Marketers—and other functions—are becoming multiskilled. Yes, to some extent, it is because of increased labor competition and a company's need to get more productivity from each resource hour spent. But it is also a natural progression of industries. As technologies and processes evolve, new skills and specializations are born while the older ones get clumped together. As mentioned before, this transition can be quite bumpy from a socioeconomic perspective, but it manifests nonetheless. Going back to the example of personal computers, we no longer have separate jobs for typists. That's a skill that may have seemed like a tall task once, but everyone has learnt it now. In a function as subdivided as marketing, the scope for clumping would be naturally higher.

As it turns out, the subfunctions of marketing are not necessarily merging with each other; they are instead doing so with different areas within the business. A diverse skillset is important also because of this latest shift in organizational structures. Earlier in our discussion, we had arrived at the onset of flat hierarchies. Thanks to remote work and virtual systems, we have also seen a growth in third-party companies and contractors who come together for a specific project.

The most common example has been the hiring of developers skilled in building machine learning models or the outsourcing of this work to companies housing many such developers available for temporary hiring. Similar is the story with sales and marketing. Since companies cannot afford too many permanent hires nor have the cycles to train and manage them, they join hands with third parties to accomplish a lead generation or demo booking project. This not only reduces their liability and risk but also brings more efficiency and cost-effectiveness.

The agility of such temporary structures has also been induced by—and bolstered in return—a fluctuating demand, giving rise to a dynamic operating model that can adapt quickly. Mass production, for example, is no longer blind to short-term changes in demand, as shown by fast fashion in clothing. Hypercustomizations—and consumer expectations of the same—are other factors that have necessitated organizations preparing for sudden shifts in demand, as was seen during the pandemic. While that implies stockpiling of inventory in some cases, it also means better prediction of demand shifts in others. And it is the marketers that must guide on both fronts.

So, most industries are saturated with competition. Demand and consumer tastes are fluctuating wildly. New markets are hard to come by. Work has gone hybrid. Data-driven decision making has become crucial.

Diverse skillset is growing in importance. And organizational structures that have existed in flat, matrix, divisional, and functional varieties are starting to adopt more agile, temporary structures. How does a marketer operate, cope, and excel in this reality?

Dessert

In this chapter, we have followed marketing from its unpretentious birth as a communication ornament, through creative adolescence of collaborative engagement, to complex maturity that harbors a sense of omnipresence—each phase led by an organization's need to differentiate itself and sustain growth in a changing competitive landscape. We touched upon why the subjectiveness of brand resonance has kept it elusive and why existing marketing silos don't help AI initiatives that innately prefer the unity of data. As shareholders, supply chains, and unforgiving customers continue to strain organizational gaps in productivity, skillsets, and costs, how can a marketer turn the tables to proactively adapt to oncoming changes in the ecosystem rather than react to them once they happen? That will be our focus in the next chapter.

CHAPTER 2

Marketing in the New Organizational Realities

Entrée

A comprehensive understanding of marketing often has two prerequisites. First is to understand the interconnectedness of marketing, sales, and customer success and how they act like one entity. Second is to understand the different elements of marketing involved in manifesting this connection—an ongoing cyclical movement of strategy reformulation and its execution. In this chapter, we will not only cover these elements but also leverage the combined knowledge from the previous chapter and this one to propose a structure that can better leverage AI to suitably predict, automate, and adapt marketing initiatives to stay ahead of the market.

The Elements of Marketing

Generative AI can be leveraged for different purposes, each occupying a specific spot in the traditional marketing workflow. It begins with a brand identity creation based on initial market research and product validation. The potential customers are then segmented to identify the most profitable one to target—a decision based on the value an offering can bring to them, and how well it can differentiate itself on that value. The outcome is an ideal customer profile (ICP) to target and a positioning to establish in their minds.

To successfully translate the positioning and ICP into revenue outcomes, the next stage defines the product and its packaging, its pricing, channels of sale, and promotional plan, all with an eye on its socioeconomic sustainability and stakeholder well-being. The latter leads to direct and indirect consideration and purchase engagements on the part of the customer. The final step in the process is the support given to the customer and the steps taken to nurture and grow that relationship.

This marketing process is often imagined linearly, with a handoff to sales and eventually to customer success. In reality, this workflow has always been cyclical because only by experiencing the customers' journey and getting their feedback can the initial research and assumptions be truly validated. Without it, any gaps in the strategy—from errors in choosing the target to deciding how to take it to market—cannot be corrected in a timely fashion.

Course correction is important because even a perfect offering can cease to be one if the market itself changes over time. It is the volume, speed, and continuity of such analyses that mandate the use of AI. As we will see, while techniques like ensemble learning can help with numeric or categorical information, making sense of subjective data is where we need generative AI.

The agility to course correct in the face of dynamically changing conditions requires early and accurate indication (or prediction) of such changes. In the age of data, every step of the customer acquisition and retention process becomes a data point that can supply crucial information and must be captured and contextually analyzed for strategic improvements.

When this author wrote the book *Modern Marketing Using AI*, which focused on the different stages of customer journeys, the workflow described above was imagined in a human form,[1] similar to BCG's generative leadership approach, which we will discuss later in this chapter. This form contained a brain, a heart, arms and legs—all connected to each other. The brain represented quantitative and qualitative data-driven insights, the heart represented the brand, online and offline selling were the arms executing revenue growth, and customer success and legal and ethical considerations were the legs.

Among these various elements, there are two we must focus on with regard to any generative AI-enabled marketing. First is the interplay of data-driven insights and the brand identity. Second is the legal and ethical considerations involved.

The interplay of insights and brand first: Deprioritizing this linkage can be crippling and has indeed led to the eventual burnout of many companies, mighty and small, who made the mistake of letting theoretical data override experiential context, or vice versa. Simply put, while data insights may recommend pursuing sales on a certain channel, the decision to pursue it and how to do so depends on its compliance with the brand identity.

Conversely, while a luxury brand may wish to stick to certain channels and audience segment, ignoring the industry' blue oceans can lead to a competitive disadvantage. Take the automobile industry: When the likes of Ford, General Motors, Toyota, or Honda had to simultaneously pursue the low-volume highly profitable luxury segment, the high-volume mass-market segment, and those in between, they all chose three completely different brands to go with for each.

Blackberry boasted an unchallenged status as an executive's darling when it came to phones. When the iPhone cracked its invincibility, the data pointed Research in Motion (RIM)—Blackberry's owner—toward the mass market audience to increase sales volumes. It would have looked logical because iPhones were relatively expensive, and the broader audience had always aspired toward owning Blackberry phones, but that was only because these phones had been the choice of executives. The aspiration was not for the phone but what it represented—wealth, power, and a leader's taste. When that changed, the mass market's taste shifted as well. Blackberry found itself in no man's land.

The legal and ethical considerations for effective marketing rarely elicit a pause. Traditionally, they hadn't been top-of-mind for marketers, a reality that saw many organizations fiddle with subliminal marketing (we will touch upon this in Part 4), creatively inaccurate statistical data, and misleading persuasive impressions. If that weren't the case, issues like lead poisoning and climate change wouldn't have been denied by some experts in the first place. After all, when "80 percent of doctors recommend" a product in a television advertisement, rarely do we hear about the number of doctors surveyed in total, which context or conditionality they spoke in, and what biases they represented. For instance, 80 percent in a group of five doctors isn't much, and it's even less meaningful if they all happen to be on a company's payroll.

Lack of concrete laws or their global standardization always allowed room for maneuvers. The first strong reckoning that marketers faced on this front was due to data and privacy. When the EU passed its General Data Protection Regulation (GDPR) law banning unsolicited e-mails to those who did not opt-in first, some of the control over the information shifted back to customers. The risks of noncompliance for organizations became real. If the domain reputation took a hit, for instance, corporate e-mails could be marked as spam and never make it to inboxes. Today, as we move increasingly toward the adoption of AI, ethics and legal compliance are becoming even more important on account of the risks they pose to customers' privacy and identity and the fact that their data is the very lifeline of this field.

They say that data is the new currency. It certainly is dictating the strategic shifts within a company. After all, if one company starts to use its brain to a higher potential, all competitors are forced to attempt the same. Our consequent dive into the depths of data is quickly revealing how every part of the marketing body can supply crucial information to compile the full story of an organizational reality, in turn necessitating newer internal touchpoints to collect more data.

Consider the case of a North American water softener company. Let's call it Silver Water. The company developed softeners that could allow homes to continuously track how hard their water was, thereby getting alerts when the softener needed more salt. Its strategy was to grab market share by solving a pressing pain point for households who otherwise had no clue how effective their softener truly was. The promotional team rolled out a hard-hitting advertisement that invoked a clear call to action: booking an initial consultation on Silver Water's website. The webform was easy and allowed customers to book a precise date and time slot to get the conversation started, thereby capitalizing on their initial excitement around the product. After several months, sales conversions remained low.

The promotional team tried tweaking the message, training the sales and support reps, and even altering the price point, but it didn't help. The company knew that customers typically had long contract periods and costly buyout clauses with their existing suppliers. Yet, the numbers were even lower than estimates. It wasn't until Silver Water started tracking the buyer journey that the true problem emerged.

The calendar setup on the website had not been aligned with those of the local distributors in each area who were supposed to send the sales reps to homes. As a result, despite a customer having booked a consultation time online, it'd take a phone call from the local distributor to find a time that actually worked for both parties. The sales reps in an area only visited households as per the schedule handed over by their distribution office and had no visibility of the times that the customer had picked originally.

The telesales or support desk at distribution offices had become a bottleneck. Despite their best attempts, most prescheduled appointments began being missed once a flood of customer enquiries started coming in as a result of the TV promotions and couldn't be manually addressed in time. The corporate office, meanwhile, had been tallying the overall volume of customer request to sales visits per month without looking at the respective dates of the two.

Customers who showed interest were primarily those nearing the end of their contract terms. Delays in talking to Silver Water meant that they were compelled to go with the best offer they could find elsewhere, initiating another lengthy contract. The sales windows were lost, and Silver Water continued to experience fewer conversions than it should have seen. This was a process issue where incomplete automation to schedule dates and to communicate to the customers in a timely fashion cost the company significantly in returns on its marketing investment.

Moral of Silver Water's story: No matter how effective each team is in meeting their respective goals, the competition is always won by companies who have the most holistic, timely, and accurate visibility across the entire value network. Is that achievable through greater collaboration between the different commercial teams? Yes, if it were served by a more suitable structural approach to marketing.

In the previous chapter, we read about two unmet demands that AI poses to every organization today:

1. First is the cross-functional and planned adoption, data and process alignment, and operational execution.
2. Second is the agility needed to quickly adapt to changing market demands and internal realities.

These requirements imply resource reallocation, goal reset, and informed stakeholders to help avoid conflicting mandates and inefficiencies in teams that reduce the overall returns. Such a need for deep and continual insights for proactive strategy formulation or course correction, and the need for agility in execution to keep pace with it are both cost and operational questions.

If we think in terms of the type of marketing tasks to accomplish, often at the scale needed, it is tough to restructure the function differently from how it currently is. A more fluid structure that meets the above needs, however, is achievable if we can find some constancy—of tasks or objectives, or both. In the case of marketing, that would be the customer journey milestones, with each step of the journey constituting one or more of three recurring task areas: **content creation, process automation, and insights generation.**

What is the essence of focusing on these three areas? A river always needs a riverbed with defined boundaries on each side for the water to flow smoothly. The same principle is true for AI models where one must start with a hypothesis—a base assumption of the solution—to then validate and evolve the model. In other words, fluidity is best achieved when it rests on some stable, unchanging condition. Finding that foundational base is key to achieving effective agile systems.

What could such a base be in marketing? In a world where markets and organizational realities are in a constant state of flux, two things remain relatively unchanging:

1. Externally, a customer's psychological journey.
2. Internally, the nature of AI tasks.

Starting with the former, most customers go through a similar psychological journey—from brand awareness to loyalty. For any brand or offering, a customer always begins by first becoming aware of it. If the awareness is positive and credible, there occurs the initial formulation of an intent to explore the offering further. Historically, engagement with the brand followed next, leading up to a purchase consideration and the actual purchase. Today, thanks to a host of online information, purchase consideration often precedes engagement, which in turn is focused on facilitating the purchase. Once a customer, both the pre- and postpurchase experience reinforces or negates an individual's initial as well as evolving expectations of the offering and the company. That eventually dictates her loyalty and longevity.

While the overall journey remains the same, different customers find themselves at different stages of the journey at any point of time. Organizational priority also tends to shift depending on its growth stage and market factors, as not all stages of the customer journey demand equal attention at all times. This is where a need for agility sets in. What remains constant is the second factor mentioned earlier: the nature of AI tasks. Regardless of the customer journey objective that a team is focused on, the AI initiatives it undertakes are likely to fall into one or more of three buckets: content creation, process automation, or insights generation.

Aligning the insights, strategy, and tasks along the customer journey allows temporary alignment along clear objectives and changing priorities, all tied to meaningful outcomes. It shifts the organization's focus and thinking from actions to results. For example, a content creator can move from seeing her work as routinely producing social media posts to one that produces content for a certain growth objective today and for another tomorrow. Instead of building a feature and trying to persuade the customer on its utility, the company can better listen to the customer, market, and other stakeholders and prioritize which established utility to fulfill.

That is how Slack went from a gaming company to an internal communication and collaboration tool. Rarely do companies abandon their main product to focus on a peripheral component like Slack did by going all-in on their handy in-game chat feature. The company did this because it was able to identify, understand, and validate a much stronger but latent customer demand that it was in a position to fulfill. Slack was worth $27.7 billion when acquired by Salesforce in 2021.

The New Marketing Structure

The idea of conceiving a new marketing structure is nothing new. As far back as 1980, a U.S. journal article on marketing issues wondered why the American marketing thinkers were "fiddling while Rome is burning" and continued to "rest on old and obsolete laurels."[2] The laurel referred to the American contribution to the marketing world by having first turned this field into a discipline. In the authors' view, marketers in Japan, Germany, and even developing nations back then had begun to outpace their counterparts in the United States without the latter realizing.

It is difficult to know when prevalent ideas start to become outdated, or others become more relevant to the present times. If that weren't true, recessions would never happen. But even as existing systems and technologies reach a breaking point, societies rarely jump to newer ones already available until things begin to collapse. Such is the nature of change—inevitable yet always resisted. Yet, as a recent paper argues, "change management in the marketing department" of a company facing external or internal factors, as we saw in the last chapter, "can be seen as an opportunity for those managers who are agile, smart and visionary."[3]

We discussed the existing organizational realities in the previous chapter. The emerging realities dictate rethinking management if we are to run an organization efficiently. Consider the consulting firm Boston Consulting Group (BCG), which has envisioned the new age of leadership in a human form, called generative leadership. Quite similar to the human form of marketing explained earlier in this chapter, BCG's generative leadership concept has three elements visualized in human form: the head, the heart, and the hands.[4] The head deals with "reimagining and reinventing the business to serve all stakeholders," the heart deals with "inspiring and enriching the human experience," and the hands deal with "executing and innovating through supercharged teams."

Why was there a need to reimagine leadership elements at all? BCG laid out several reasons, many on the lines of the internal and external forces discussed earlier, including artificial intelligence (AI). These were complex and high stakes issues in uncertain times that necessitated generative leadership. The philosophy of leading with head, heart and hands essentially encapsulated business transformation, being purpose-driven—an attribute that BCG says results in 8 percent less turnover and a twofold increase in productivity—and ensuring "agility across boundaries."

A need for agility is also what the aforementioned paper on change management stressed upon. That paper expressed that such considerations apply even more in marketing as "the rate of change is much faster than ever before" in this department.[5] The question, therefore, is: How can leaders reimagine and reinvent their organization to make it purpose-led and agile in a way that gets the most out of AI? One solution is to break the walls that impede this behavior and reduce AI's effectiveness.

Today, we have product marketing, demand generation, social media marketing, channel management, and a host of others that all carry components that can be automated, generate insights that are not shared quickly enough, and harbor conflicting goals and motivations. Companies have encountered crippling inefficiencies trying to bring together their current silos. These can involve—though are not limited to—misleading or incongruent insights, an inability to generate them, severe resource limitations in the absence of automation (even in large organizations), and stack fatigue due to uneven overautomation.

Siloed scaling initiatives don't work because they are inward-looking and somewhat myopic. It is why over 90 percent of start-ups fail, and those that survive have to readjust their strategy. Take funded start-ups in the software industry as an example. They are often faced with immense growth targets due to investor pressures. One of the valuation components deals with aggressive product roadmaps. Most start-ups, flush with fresh investments, go on a hiring spree to turbocharge their product evolution, sales, and support. It typically leads to bulky solutions that do not necessarily resonate with customers, necessitating user interface and user experience (UI/UX) focus to drive stickiness with the product. However, with decreasing resonance value, sales and customer retention pressures continue to mount, and the initial flood of hiring almost always gives way to mass layoffs.

The underlying challenge remains the same in each case—a structure not set up to leverage or be driven by AI fast enough to keep pace with the market demands. AI doesn't work best in silos. That is true for two reasons: silos limit the comprehensiveness and usefulness of insights generated, and they create resource bottlenecks that limit how much timely execution can be done.

According to a *Harvard Business Review* article, scaling generative AI requires a certain type of focus. That includes enabling explorers of this technology, focusing on building platforms instead of individual or disconnected AI products, and prioritizing the impact of AI initiatives.[6]

Maximizing results from the available resources in the age of AI mandates such a structural rethink. The front-runners of the AI reality understand this need, which is perhaps why in a Deloitte Digital survey, 72 percent of respondents said that they were consolidating marketing insights and measurement teams into a single group within the marketing function.[7]

How does insights consolidation help? It enables 360-degree insights encompassing all related areas of operations, customer touchpoints, and market dynamics. An AI-ready structure has other attributes as well. It allows seamless automation that can capture as much of the information and process flow as possible from one step or system to another, so people don't have to spend their precious time doing that instead. It is also dependent on effective human resource management—in generating content that is needed to armor the automation steps at scale, and that follows a clear strategic direction based on the insights coming in real time. All of this ensures that people understand the role they play in a larger vision, and can see how their work aligns with—and contributes to—the overall goal. They can also be agile enough to course correct when needed, without losing sight of the big picture.

This is a very different structural setup, constituting three functions and several dynamic project areas or teams. In an agile organization trying to adapt to uncertain changes in the market, a lack of rigid structures—functional, divisional, or matrix—can be a good thing. It is a reality where teams or individuals from within and outside the organization should be able to assemble to meet certain goals and flow separately into other goal pursuits simultaneously or once the prior goal is achieved. This fluidity is aided by the application of contactless services, seamless flow of information, and more contextual awareness of the bigger picture surrounding an initiative. How does such an AI-driven, agile, and effective marketing organization look?

In the following image (Figure 2.1), the three new marketing functions are—content, automation, and insights. These are the three forms of execution involved in achieving most marketing objectives, particularly when leveraging AI. These three core groups feed resources into marketing project areas which focus on different aspects of any customer journey—from strategy to promotions to sales and support. The number

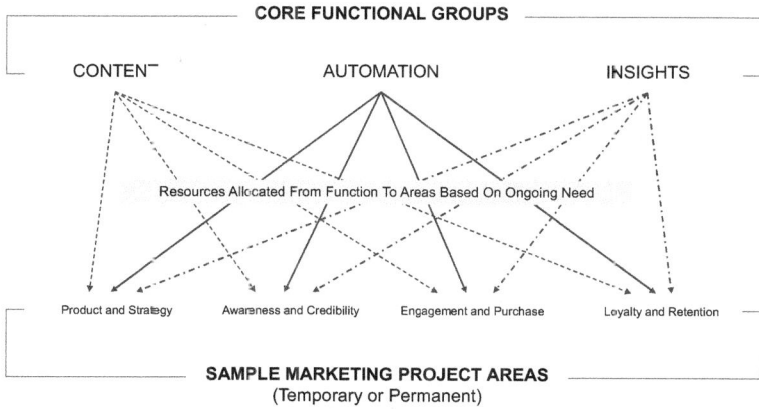

Figure 2.1 Organizational structure for AI-driven marketing

of resources from the three core groups in each of the project areas can be adjusted as the priority and demands of a project area change with time. In fact, project areas can even be created or dissolved as per need. There is a fourth group that can become more third-party sourced if needed: the frontline workers. We will discuss that logic in more detail in Part 3 of this book when we dive into how the three functional groups can better leverage AI to execute specific objectives with the frontline, whether it's the salespeople or the call center agents. For now, let's get an introductory overview of each group.

The Content Functional Group

The content group is where the AI content generators sit, but these are not just artists. Content refers to all information that populates systems, is utilized by others in the organization, and is shared internally or externally. For example, it can include legal, policy, or training documents that need to be fed into a generative AI model for certain parties to quickly procure the information they need.

This group also constitutes the prompt engineers generating anything from images for social media to program codes for a new model or website. In that sense, this group comprises subject matter experts across technical, creative, and other areas.

Content strategy is not the same as tactics. The latter deals with initiatives that resources from this group can execute in the project areas they are allotted to. This functional group governs the overall strategy based on clear objectives and a holistic understanding (and visibility) of content across the organization, the requirements it has of other groups, and the role it occupies in fulfilling their requirements in return.

The Automation Functional Group

The automation team is the next evolution of current operational teams, tasked with ensuring all AI and non-AI systems are planned and work in tandem. Based on an overarching understanding of the complete process needed to execute the planned strategy, this team envisions how different parts of the process within the project areas can be automated and integrated to auto-communicate with each other.

At this point, most of us tend to fear job displacement, for good reason. While that is certainly a possibility, it is not a necessity. That possibility has played out since the Industrial Revolution, but good automations more often tend to make our jobs easier by taking away the mundane and repetitive tasks that make us unproductive and cause errors.

Think about a salesperson. Would she rather be out selling or filling in customer data on a CRM (customer relationship management) software? Even for someone in telesales, would they rather be cold calling random people all day to gauge interest or focusing on calling those who have already shown some signals of interest? Even in factories, AI is likely to be no different in the impact its preceding techno-economic evolutions have had, but it can at least allow greater safety and reallocation of workers to supervisory and safer working environments.

Automation is also often interpreted as a one-time job. Once you have set up a system, what else is there to do? A lot, as it turns out. Ask any systems administrator and they would tell you that systems are never failproof. Something always breaks down, needs adjustment or can create issues in terms of redundancies or bottlenecks. While the initial setup itself is a massive undertaking, its continual success depends on close managerial eyes. If that were not the case, companies would not need software developers once a software was built and ready.

The Insights Functional Group

Finally, the insights group is responsible for capturing and consolidating insights from all areas and formulating or revising the strategy. This is where AI-savvy strategists sit. Today, insight generation rests with systems administration teams or internal operations who juggle between managing the systems and processes and capturing and communicating the insights, which causes lapses in what information is relayed higher up and delays in how quickly it is relayed. Almost always, context is missing for the upper management devising the next course of action based on these insights.

Timing is crucial. After all, why are AI systems tasked with real-time analyses—from live in-game data in sports to ongoing transaction fraud alerts at banks? It is because insights needed to prevent your identity theft or to assess the playing opponent's strategy cannot wait till your credit card has already been misused or the game is already over, respectively.

Organizational super-power is unleashed when holistic insights are generated and analyzed as they come in. AI will enable organizations to achieve this in more and more areas of work. Without dedicated insights personnel, one cannot expect different teams to accomplish such speed while working separately.

So, how do these three functional groups work together to accomplish revenue growth responsibly?

The Project Teams

The three functional groups of subject matter experts, operators, and strategists described earlier feed resources into projects as needed, giving the organization the agility it needs. For starters, resources from these functions come together to work on specific objectives which are set along the customer journey milestones that any company must achieve for an offering. The specific project areas and their permanence can be decided and altered by the organization. As an example, one could start with four broad areas in marketing: product and strategy, awareness and credibility, engagement and purchase, and retention and growth. It can then break these further or change them as its needs change. That flexibility is the big boon of converting these traditional sub functions into project areas.

Depending on the organizational size, outsourced and internal resources from each of the content, automation, and insights areas are continuously or occasionally engaged to work in one or more of these projects.

How is this setup more fluid and more timely than current marketing structures? As mentioned previously, projects based on customer journey milestones are ongoing but can be prioritized or deprioritized as organizational realities change. Since they are not fixed teams, each project can move from being resource-heavy to resource-light as needed. For instance, Nestlé may not need to build brand awareness anymore, just to maintain it. However, in the event of a new product launch or a reputational crisis, as seen with its palm oil controversy, it can shift more resources to Awareness or Credibility projects quickly.

Agility is not the only benefit here; effectiveness is another. In AI-driven organizations, we need resources who understand and can manage AI to achieve specific use cases. Those equipped to generate content with generative AI can do so for any project objective they are called for. Marketers can then carry an overall understanding of the different aspects of marketing and specialize instead on the executional variety. As we discussed in the earlier chapter, that is the kind of skill change that is being driven by our techno-economic evolution.

How else can this help organizations? Instead of specializing in one subarea of marketing, resources from the three groups bring three valuable elements to any project they are a part of.

First, they carry an informed 360-view of the organizational reality and context in their functional area. This is because information can be readily shared when someone carrying insights on customer feedback from the Retention project area belongs to the same Insights function as someone involved in strategizing product features in the Product area, both reporting to their function leader—the Head of the Insights group, who is in charge of ensuring all areas are informed and aligned.

Second, such resources can adapt and apply that knowledge to their respective project goals and communicate updates back to their functional area, from where it trickles to the other projects, thereby keeping everyone informed. Such a quaquaversal view helps avoid actionability on limited information in any one project.

Third, this structure enables better policy formulation and governance to ensure policy adherence, as each project is graced with experts that have a better understanding of a certain facet of AI and are in a better position to assess ethical behaviors, job risks, or legal liabilities with regard to a planned deployment.

Dessert

We have now revisited the various elements involved in marketing that can be enhanced with generative AI and have also seen why these elements operating separately come in the way of doing so efficiently today. This chapter has proposed a structural reset that allows feeder functions—based on three core areas of any AI usage—to dynamically equip projects that follow specific marketing objectives. In doing so, it achieves a much-needed real-time collaboration across the marketing organization while allowing quicker adaptability to market requirements. We will discuss how this new structure helps marketing better leverage generative AI and manage resources and overall costs in Part 3. However, to appreciate that nuance, it is important to first understand AI and its requirements better. How radical or obvious one finds the proposed marketing structure depends on how familiar one is with AI's successes and failures in organizations. So, it is time to dive into a mini crash course on this topic.

PART 2

AI Unlocked

To improve is to change; To be perfect is to change often.

—Winston Churchill

An example I often cite to drive home AI's importance to our careers is that of Microsoft Office. Back in the 90s, MS Office did not seem like a mandatory tool to familiarize oneself with. It became one over time. Today, you are expected to know how to use Word, PowerPoint, or Excel. That, however, does not mean that you've had to learn how to build these applications, only to understand what they can and cannot do and to leverage them. That is the trajectory AI is on.

Artificial intelligence (AI) started with statistical ingenuity. Similar to the organizational evolution we discussed in Part 1, evolving needs and newer challenges powered iterations that eventually led to the impressive generative AI we use today. Having looked at the kind of tasks it involves, and before we delve into how to use these tools for marketing, it is important to understand the technology itself and what it needs. That is our focus over the next three chapters.

In the first chapter of Part 2, we will imbibe the central tenets of AI and what, specifically, generative AI is. Managerial relevance will remain our guiding star as we then discuss the steps typically involved in AI journeys in organizations. The first part of that narrative will look at factors involved in initiating AI journeys. The second part will look at those that govern how an organization should go about AI deployments and usage.

CHAPTER 3

From Statistics to Generative AI

Entrée

Artificial intelligence can sound both fascinating and scary to those looking to better understand the technology. We often miss the realization that the bulk of a workforce does not need to code; just understand the techniques conceptually. This chapter attempts to achieve the latter for the reader by unlocking the basics of AI and the rationale underlying its many techniques in use today. Starting with augmented statistics, we will see how each technique serves as a foundation for something more complex, eventually leading to the advanced human-like capabilities that mesmerize us today.

Artificial intelligence is an umbrella term for computer programs that operate on advanced statistical principles to do four things. They receive inputs, analyze them, and provide outputs—fairly standard programming tasks so far—but they also learn from the past to improve with time.

AI's learning can be supervised or unsupervised. Human supervision, though, can lead to two issues. First, it can introduce biases—obvious or hidden. Second, it can limit AI's capability to what humans can conceive. The capability referred to here is one of pattern recognition, which in many ways feeds all intelligence—natural and artificial. This is why the more advanced AI systems get, the more they lean toward being unsupervised, which is where most of our fears around this technology come from.

It is natural for us to fear something intelligent enough to grasp that which we cannot. The same prehistoric genes that ordained the skill of pattern recognition upon us are also responsible for the fear we feel with something new that we do not fully understand. Our first assumption is always that this new entity will harm us. It is the biological balancing act to keep us safe and steady in our progress. But trying to dominate over when given a chance is a very human way of thinking about what another intelligent entity may do. If we observe the creation around us, we will find that's not true for everything.

The sun utterly dominates the earth in size and power but does not destroy it. In fact, it nurtures the planet. The trees vastly outnumber and have outlasted humans, but they haven't set out to harm us either. The bacteria on and inside our bodies outnumber us by trillions but maintain a symbiotic relationship of mutualism. Even creatures around us that we claim superiority over—from dogs to dolphins—are intelligent enough to understand what we say (even though we don't necessarily understand what they are saying!) and could overpower many of us physically, but they don't.

Ninety-nine percent of all species that have ever lived on earth never foresaw their end. So, to imagine possibilities of threat at every step is a survival mechanism—an important one. But the danger AI really poses to our species has more to do with the fact that it is our creation, not nature's. As such, it is bound by our flaws and motivations. In other words, the threat AI poses is first and foremost from us not understanding what it is and how it works, because by not understanding the technology well, we leave it blindly in the hands of those who do and who may use it for their own benefit at the cost of others.

In all fairness, self-defense has always been a strong motivator for life to take aggressive action. AI itself was born from the cradle of World War II when supercharged mathematics was the need of the hour to outsmart the enemy and survive. We have come a long way in under a century since then, and much like the universe's expansion, AI's expansion is accelerating as well. Understanding why AI has evolved the way it has can instantly instill an understanding of which techniques to use when.

The analysis AI models run are broadly meant to find patterns in the data. It is a skill that has guided human progress since ancient times. Repeated patterns of pain or fatalities are how cavemen identified the dangers of veering out after dark, interacting with wild animals or eating certain berries. Repetitive patterns are also how babies learn not to go close to the fire, basketball players learn how to shoot accurately, and auto-insurance firms learn which drivers may be more prone to accidents.

The challenge has always been to find useful patterns. Many could simply be irrelevant or hidden, leading us to rely on misleading data. There is a reason why the earth was once considered the center of our solar system. We don't know what we don't know. To discover all the patterns that exist in a certain situation is akin to discovering all the galaxies that exist in the universe with our bare eyes. It may be possible theoretically, but in practice, we will never know for sure. More importantly, the time it takes us and the errors that could creep in would render the exercise not very useful or worth undertaking. In such a case, using a machine like the Hubble Telescope can help us far more than it can hurt us.

Let's say a product marketer of a shaving razor company sets out to accurately profile her current and potential customers. It may be easy to get their demographic data and purchase history but the deeper she goes into understanding variations in customer behaviors and nature, the more subjective and elusive data become. Even with a sound understanding of when Sam buys a shaving razor and what factors underlie his choice, how will she ever know if she knows enough to predict any change in Sam's behavior in the future?

The answer requires analyzing data that are large enough to uncover deeply hidden patterns where Sam's choice of razor could depend on 20 different factors, including his partner's fascination with organic juice! The rationale could be that Sam's partner buys organic juice at a specific retail chain, which only sells a particular brand of razors that she then buys for Sam when she goes shopping. In other words, not Sam but his partner is now the effective customer. Trying to get that level of detail is what propelled us to superpower statistics.

The Onset of Machine Learning

Patterns have long been the domain of statisticians. Reflect on a basic technique like regression. Let's say we plot a price-demand graph for a birthday card, where the market demand for the card goes down as its price increases. If one imagines a scatter plot—a graph plotting the demand volume at increasing price points—one is likely to notice a line mostly sloping downwards from left to right. Say, the graph shows a reduction in demand when the price increases from $20 to $30. It would be easy to extend this line to estimate how low the demand would go when the price reaches $35. Predicting demand by recognizing a straightforward pattern in this case is the earliest and simplest example of the foundations of AI.

When a need arose to consider multiple factors (other than just the price) to gauge and predict demand volumes, statistics evolved to incorporate techniques like multiple linear regression. But while basic software could tackle such analyses with a lot of data, thereby powering early market researchers, it faced an inherent limitation. Statistical software was reasonably effective only when the statistician knew which parameters to consider to solve a problem. As consumer behavior—and other such use cases—became more subjective and the drivers of purchase decisions were unknown, we needed to go past this statistical limitation. That led to the birth of machine learning.

Machine learning was the next stage of AI which still banked on known statistical techniques but had a key difference: it figured out the analyses itself, by looking at the inputs and outputs to identify patterns between them. As we discussed before, patterns are best found when there is sufficient data. Suddenly, data became important for the richness or depth of patterns that could be surfaced.

Classification and regression techniques remained the backbone of analyses but they were upgraded to something called ensemble learning. It was a technique where—with ample data—a machine learning model could not only map many more patterns and subpatterns but also validate them and course correct as it went forward.

Decision trees was a common approach. A model would look at one parameter—say, whether Sam has a partner—and check Sam's razor choice with or without one. If a partner existed, the model would then look at the price bucket Sam goes for. For a given price bucket, it would then look at the day and time of purchase. Weekday purchases just after workday could mean that Sam buys a certain brand on the way back from work, while weekend purchases when Sam is with his partner could mean a different brand altogether. Machine learning was required to identify the relevant patterns—and the order in which they should be analyzed—from a wide variety of information available on Sam.

One way of superpowering such decision *trees* with dependent branches—one springing from another—was by creating a *forest* of multiple trees. That was the birth of the random forest technique, which eventually powered Microsoft's Xbox and gave consumers the ability to play video games like tennis with hand gestures—all movements being simultaneously mapped and predicted to allow an opponent's response.

Machine learning also had other techniques at its disposal. While classification could predict categories (nonnumerical data such as Sam's weekend anomaly), clustering could help group other customers like Sam in one behavioral bucket, association rule learning could help determine an association between the purchase of razors and organic juice on weekends, Monte Carlo simulation could help estimate the risk of such predictions being incorrect, and search algorithms could help find the shortest route to a predicted outcome. That last one became the original darling of Google, of course, and gave way to e-commerce platforms where users could search for a product from a massive online catalog.

Advanced Problems, Advanced Solutions

Despite the advances, the parameters driving an outcome in the real world could still only be partially known or could change over time. Since machine learning models relied on historical data of which set of inputs led to which outputs, any change in the reality would take time for the model to learn and adapt to. How could learning happen in real time? Not every use case afforded the luxury of delayed action, as we discussed in the case of credit card fraud or advertisement efficiency.

One step in the right direction came with gamification, thanks to a technique called reinforcement learning. The model would allocate points for a correct prediction—say, in choosing a social media post that customers would like more—and deduct them for incorrect ones. As time progressed and more customers engaged with the different variations of a social media post, the system would start to prioritize the best-performing one. That is why most social media channels today ask for multiple images and headline combinations when we launch an online advertisement.

One other distinct use case that required solving was that of communication. While the data being analyzed so far was tabular and could be bucketed into specific parameters, what about regular conversations? Natural language processing (NLP) helped devise a way to break down sentences and other such text into tabulated data, where certain words could be bucketed together. Different buckets represented emotion, tone, subject, object, and so on, which could then be classified just as any dataset would be. This was the first step toward a program having real conversations.

AI had reached its limits in the types of tasks it could do. Anything beyond this required an ability to uncover deeper and more complex patterns. That required analyzing many more parameters and a much larger volume of data. How could one train a model to do that? The answer, as with the best of inventions in human history, was provided by nature.

The brains of advanced organisms excel in processing huge volumes of data every second. They do so with the help of neurons—nodes connected to and relaying information to each other where relevant information is procured to make sense of a situation. The same logic led to the creation of deep learning. Figure 3.1 shows a sample of how our brain's approach of neural networks is replicated in the case of AI.

Deep learning worked on the principle of having multiple layers of neural nodes. In the first layer, each node represented a parameter that may be relevant to predicting an outcome (say, Sam's choice of razors). Another layer of nodes would receive different combinations of these parameters. So, instead of testing which parameters were more important one by one, the nodes could simultaneously try different weightages assigned to each parameter (say, day and time, price, Sam's relationship

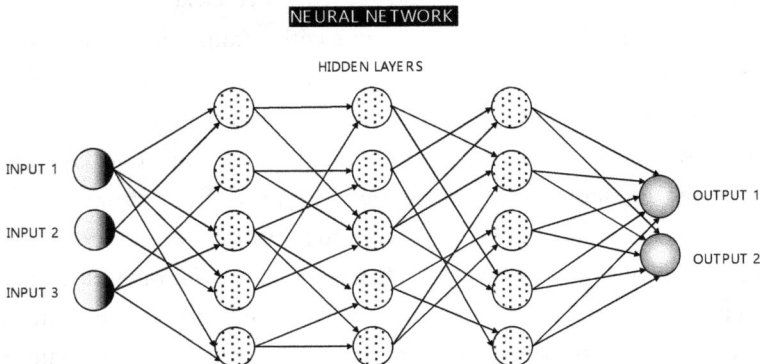

NEURAL NETWORK

HIDDEN LAYERS

INPUT 1
INPUT 2
INPUT 3

OUTPUT 1
OUTPUT 2

Figure 3.1 A sample neural network

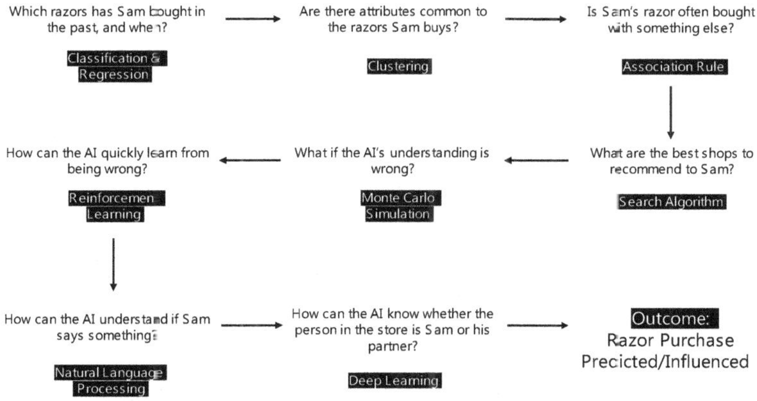

Figure 3.2 A snapshot of AI techniques

status, etc.). These nodes would relay different combinations of factors (read: inputs) to another layer of nodes, and so on. The output would then be tested against actual outcomes of Sam's choice historically to self-correct or confirm which set of nodes best represents reality.

These many techniques that make up the foundations of AI models are good to grasp—even if only at a conceptual level—for anyone looking to leverage AI in their organizations. While they can be further learnt at ClassesAI.com or in the book *Artificial Intelligence for Managers*, our focus in this book is generative AI. For now, Figure 3.2 shows a snapshot of how the different techniques could work in tandem.

The Birth of Generative AI

The net result of the neural network approach was an enhancement in AI's ability to perform tasks that had an unknown and more complex set of parameters at play. Chief among these new use cases was the ability to *see*, also known as image recognition.

Large volumes of data could now be assessed to reveal unforeseen patterns and accomplish more subjective-looking tasks. Consumers could be profiled much more deeply, to an extent where the AI knew about their inherent nature and could predict behaviors even before they became consciously aware of it. We had now arrived at two new challenges to take the next step. The first challenge was the time it would take to process such large amounts of data. That was a costly affair, only afforded by large organizations with ample resources and a vast database. The second challenge was the need to have a vast set of data in the first place.

The first problem was solved with a new architectural setup—called the transformer architecture. It followed an approach called attention mechanism which, simply put, was to impart models the ability to develop a memory. Random access memory (RAM) had long been used to make computers faster by helping them utilize short-term memory of data. In the case of the attention mechanism, neural networks were taught to remember the data they had processed previously so as to not restart the analyses from scratch each time. It led to the development of foundation models which could process data far more quickly, thereby allowing engagement and output in real time. And that was the birth of generative AI. Figure 3.3 shows these foundation model layers.

Unpacking the logical layers of
Foundation Models (FM)

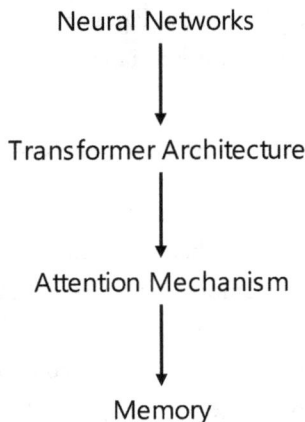

Neural Networks

↓

Transformer Architecture

↓

Attention Mechanism

↓

Memory

Figure 3.3 Typical layers of foundation models

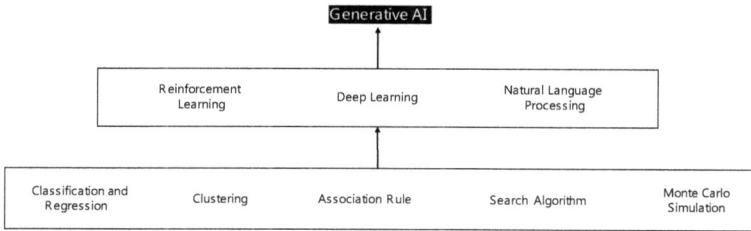

Figure 3.4 Hierarchical complexity of AI techniques

Coupled with the conversational technique of NLP, it led us to the fascinating world of ChatGPT. With image recognition based on deep learning's convolutional neural networks (CNN), it produced DALL-E, the AI artist. And with reinforcement learning, it opened up autonomous driving possibilities where a car could better see the traffic and roads, navigate, and course correct in real time. Figure 3.4 shows the major AI techniques in terms of their hierarchical complexity.

The next remaining challenge (for now) is the need for large datasets. It also leads us to the amazingly promising and risky use cases that would come with it, all of which we will deal with in the last part of this book as it looks at the future.

Dessert

Fears associated with AI always demand rectification, but this chapter also discussed what makes AI inevitable and necessary to sustain competitiveness. In deconstructing what underlies the intelligent entity we seem to be creating, we have progressed from the ancient technique of visible pattern recognition to tracing invisible patterns that allow us to predict ever-greater details of the future. Generative AI is powerful because it brings together linguistic analysis, self-learning, and the ability to process information the way a human brain does. But while it can work in tandem with other techniques, these are not always prepackaged tools that one can simply plug into any use case. So, our next step is to discuss some of the managerial thumb rules a marketer must follow to leverage AI solutions.

CHAPTER 4

Managing AI Journeys— Part 1

Entrée

A deluge of AI experts has granted us the luxury of enjoying robust models suited to any unique use case our organization may have. Yet, it is not the models but their management where returns on investment tend to become evasive. Initiating AI journeys entails several components—from checking an organization's readiness to use AI, given its requirements, to the very decision of whether to use AI to solve a problem. These two front-end assessments will be covered in this chapter before we move to the others in the next one.

Baseball is not the fastest sport by a mile, but it can make for an intense affair. Despite nine innings of play, one hit falling short of the fence by mere inches can turn a four-run homer into naught. The careful build-up, a spate of luck, timely substitutions, misplays, and all strategies leading to a scoring opportunity can go waste, and a team may never recover. And despite a Major League Baseball season of 160-plus games, that one mishit could be the difference between a team that makes the playoffs and one that doesn't.

With margins for error being deceptively low, the 2011 movie *Moneyball* revealed how the game shifted from being led primarily by subjective on-field decisions to off-the-field programmed calculations. Fast forward to 2023, and the Toronto Blue Jays had squeezed into the postseason playoffs but were now one game away from being eliminated by the Minnesota Twins. In this do-or-die game, they experienced three great innings pitched by Jose Berrios but replaced him unexpectedly in the fourth, only to concede runs and eventually lose the game. Starting pitchers on a good run typically last through six or seven innings. So, what happened?

One speculation was that the data showed that bringing a left-handed pitcher in Yusei Kikuchi could have led the Twins to bring in their right-handed batters earlier in the game, which in turn would work well for the Blue Jays' mid-to-late inning pitching line-up of right-handed pitchers that were to follow.[1] In this knockout game though, they conceded two runs soon after the change and could not recover.

The team's thinking process that day cannot be known definitively, of course, but the strategic change could easily have been hailed as heroic if things had gone their way. Even as a hypothetical scenario, the thinking above does exemplify the benefit and pitfalls of data-driven actions. It takes us back to our initial discussion on the importance of identifying multiple parameters that influence an outcome—but acknowledging the limits of not knowing whether we have identified enough parameters. In practice, that necessitates keeping context in mind while making data-driven decisions.

In the speculative scenario above, for instance, if one right-handed pitcher is already doing well, the assumption that others that come after may not is a big one to make. If one chooses to stick with this assumption regardless and risk conceding runs with an early pitching change, one must also assume that the batters will be able to outscore their opponents eventually. Assumptions make anything a game of probability, and the probability of an outcome always reduces as the number of assumptions increases.

So how do we hop over such pitfalls to minimize business risks when it comes to AI investments? Most organizations encounter failed investments despite using a robust AI model primarily because of a lack of readiness, understanding or fit with the organizational needs and its realities. This is why managing AI journeys carefully is important. Let's start by looking at two crucial elements of initiating AI journeys: checking one's readiness levels and deciding whether to invest in AI at all.

AI and Data Readiness

AI readiness is a crucial first step for any organization, which is why most companies are coming up with a readiness assessment tool of their own. These assessments can focus on one or more of a variety of topics, including:

1. Governance and ethics;
2. Data;
3. AI maturity (process and systems);
4. AI skills and culture;
5. Strategy (e.g., the AI Strategy Scorecard, created by Professor Andy Pardoe);
6. Specific verticals, functions, or use cases (e.g., Salesforce's AI Readiness Index for Government or TTEC's AI Readiness for CX); and
7. AI models/technologies (e.g., the Foundation Model Transparency Index launched by the Stanford Center for Research on Foundation Models).

Among these, data and process readiness often go together because the latter enables the former, and accountabilities have to be set for each. If one looks closely at organizations attempting an AI journey, most will appear caught not in building or buying AI models but in a data clean-up and delineation exercise.

They say 70 percent of a data scientist's time goes into data preprocessing rather than building and testing an AI model. Preprocessing here refers to readying the data to be understood and accurately analyzed by a model. That includes labeling and encoding the data properly, adding any missing information, and scaling the different types of data to be comparable. For example, what if data in imperial units were fed into a system that understood metric units? The result could be costly, as NASA found out when it lost its $125 million Mars Climate Orbiter to a similar error of conversion![2]

The better the state of data collection and management, the more adaptable it will be to different models. What does *better* imply here? As a thumb rule, we can use the TUSCANE approach[3] here. The seven letters in this acronym point at seven key requirements of data readiness, stating that the data should be timely, usable, structured, complete, accurate, not biased, and enough in volume.

These conditions are not always easy to meet and are often contextual but serve as a good navigation point for marketers taking stock of the information that is available for analysis. Among these, the need for data to be structured is probably the one where most progress has been made, as advanced AI techniques are starting to rely less and less on this condition. Nonetheless, as it is with an organized office desk, some degree of structure does make one more efficient.

How can a marketer ensure that the right internal and external data is captured to meet the aforementioned conditions? Three elements factor in here: vision, system, and people.

Vision refers to an understanding of the kind of data that is important. There is no dearth of variables that can be captured, but capturing and managing them can come at a cost. Consider a sales team asking its people to painstakingly record details on every customer interaction and sales opportunity. While more data is good, the more time a salesperson spends entering data, the less time she will spend selling. On the other hand, as we saw with the example of the water softener earlier in the book, if data is not accurately captured to reflect what goes on between a customer showing interest in the first interaction and making the actual purchase, critical insights may be lost.

This brings us to the system consideration. Data reveal dependencies between different areas of the business in driving growth, but these areas can use different systems to store data. As a result, even common data points may be difficult to reconcile if, say, company names are logged as Account in one database and as Organization in another, or New York shows up with its full name in one and as NY in another. Distinct systems aside, even the same CRM platform can have multiple instances within a company, each with its own workflow and fields.

Marketers aiming to lead with AI-driven insights should maintain a data dictionary, complete with an accompanying RACI framework. It can detail, among other things, the different types of data being captured, where it's needed, its dependencies, timing and usage within the organization, and the people who are responsible and accountable for its upkeep as well those to be consulted and kept informed.

Structures like the one above help marketers stay on top of their data and have all stakeholders aligned to fix any issues therein or to avoid them altogether.

Build or Buy AI

A courier company operating at capacity needed to start declining more and more of the shipment orders coming from its business customers. The customer order details rested in a different system than the one that carried the cost of shipping those orders. These costs also took time to calculate as they came in only once the shipments had been successfully delivered. Under the circumstances, the volume of orders being placed traditionally dictated the company's default approach to deciding which customers to say no to.

The natural thesis was that customers giving more business should take priority at the expense of others. Profitability, though, remained low. Upon further investigation, the company found that in a price-sensitive market, hypernegotiations meant that the larger customers also enjoyed steeper discounts. Their orders were also more complex and therefore, costlier to deal with. As a result, the courier company was incurring losses on most orders from some of its biggest buyers while exhausting all its capacity on them!

Profit is a factor of revenue and costs. With neither data available in real time when an order was placed, how could the company start prioritizing accounts better? There was no prebuilt solution in the market for such a problem. The company brought in third-party data science experts but assigned its own team to minimize the steep learning curve that outsiders would have to go through on the realities of the business.

This million-dollar initiative was a bold one—to build a predictive AI model that could predict profitability on a customer order without looking at the financial data. No revenues, no costs, only the categorical information surrounding the orders was looked at. The resulting model empowered the company to better negotiate orders with the loss-making enterprise accounts and to avoid losing those who had earlier seemed unattractive despite their high profitability potential. The net result was an over 200 percent return on investment in the first year alone.

Building or buying a capability is the eternal choice that eventually leads to consolidations in a mature market. In the case of AI, it's not simply a matter of having the right talent. The choice typically depends on the overall cost-benefit ratio. Costs here fall into three categories: financial, personnel, and process. While financial costs would include the outright investment as well as the sunk and opportunity costs, personnel costs refer to hiring, upskilling, and loss of jobs. Process costs, meanwhile, relate to stack fatigue, interrupted processes, and redundancies that can be introduced in a company's operational realities, particularly if one AI system doesn't sit well with others already in place.

The benefits with regard to AI are generally one or more of five types. An AI model can make solving a problem quicker, cheaper, easier, or possible where it wasn't before. Besides these, it can also solve the problem in a better way in terms of its collateral impact and other opportunities that it opens up. A great example here is that of Notion Labs, Inc., which offers a connected workspace to bring all productivity-enhancing tasks in one place. Generative AI helped it develop a writing assistant, which quickly became its own product in Notion's suite.[4]

The build-or-buy decision making can be structured around an internal assessment called FAB.[5] FAB stands for find, answer, and build. It refers to the three levels of assessments that go into a build-or-buy decision:

1. Finding comparable solutions in the market for a use case to assess the organization's data, talent, and systems readiness to use AI.
2. Answering whether AI is the best investment for your use case, given what is available in the market to buy and your readiness levels to leverage them.
3. Building a proof-of-concept to qualify the build option if AI is needed and buying a tool is not a clear option.

The quicker we validate our AI readiness and, if needed, the feasibility of building an AI model, the lower our investment risk and opportunity costs will be in deciding whether to use AI at all and, if so, whether to build or buy one.

Dessert

One of the most potent ways to establish an approach is to present them in relatable formats. While TUSCANE may be only phonetically similar to the popular Italian region, it does help understand the essentials that deem organizational datasets ready to be used by AI. That, however, is only one initial component of the FAB approach, which aims to structure a marketer's assessment of whether AI can present the most cost-effective and rewarding solution to a business problem and if so, whether to build or buy one. Yet, effective management of AI solutions does not stop here. There are other risks to look at, policies to formulate, and processes and measures to put in place to ensure the solution works the way it was intended to. Let us now turn our attention to these.

CHAPTER 5

Managing AI Journeys— Part 2

Entrée

Having checked the AI readiness levels and decided whether to invest in AI, we begin to deploy our chosen solution and drive its adoption within the organization. Before we embark on that journey, we must understand the risks that AI brings and establish certain guidelines to manage them. This is also important for successful ROI generation. How success is defined needs clarity across the organization, which necessitates finalizing the metrics to measure AI and its users' performance. And, of course, the deployment journey itself has a few nuances to take care of for a smooth adoption curve. This chapter covers it all.

AI Risks

When ChatGPT was launched to much fanfare, it unleashed a race among companies to gain or preserve competitive advantage. Generative AI had managed to induce this FOMO-led excitement where its ancestors had failed, primarily due to how familiar and humanlike it made AI to the masses. There was no longer a learning curve required for the users, and all of what one imagined AI to be—a talking robot—seemed to be coming true.

Yet, it was only a matter of months when Amazon reportedly discovered generative AI responses that were eerily similar to its internal data.[*] It quickly issued an alert to its users to avoid sharing confidential information

---

[*] www.businessinsider.com/amazon-chatgpt-openai-warns-employees-not-share-confidential-information-microsoft-2023-1

with ChatGPT. Samsung followed suit, as did many major U.S. banks,[†] all moving to limit the risks of losing sensitive and proprietary information to the Web. Surprisingly enough, even Microsoft—a key investor in OpenAI which owns ChatGPT—restricted its employees' use of ChatGPT for a while at one point owing to security and data concerns![‡]

AI inherently brings risks that companies and their leaders must guard against. There are typically seven types: systems, jobs, dependencies, data access, security, legal, and accuracy-related risks.

The systems and job-related risks correspond to the impact of an AI tool on existing processes and resources within the company. Introduction of an AI solution can hamper both. Every solution requires its own supporting processes, and if these do not align with others in place, the collateral impact is inefficiency and resource wastage. A bigger collateral impact, of course, is the existing jobs on the line, at least until new ones get created to fill the worker void. While automation often moves workers from performing a task to managing the automation of that task, poor planning can cost a company in terms of employee churn if disillusionment and insecurity compel people to move to other companies.

It can be difficult to adjudge the potential impact of AI on jobs. One way is to estimate how much of any given job deals with tasks that are not mission-critical, do not require intuitive elements, follow certain rules, and experience minimal unexpected situations. To test how susceptible a job may be to AI automation, you can visit AIJobCalculator.com.

Dependencies are another area related to the introduction of AI solutions. Even for ones that work well, an organization should also watch out for becoming over-reliant on assets controlled by third parties. It can have grave cost repercussions in the future, and any loss of control over processes and tools critical for operational growth can make the organization vulnerable to market changes or even to strategic moves by those third-party vendors.

[†] www.forbes.com/sites/siladityaray/2023/05/02/samsung-bans-chatgpt-and-other-chatbots-for-employees-after-sensitive-code-leak/

[‡] www.cnbc.com/2023/11/09/microsoft-restricts-employee-access-to-openais-chatgpt.html

Data access and security risks refer directly to the information accessible to an AI solution. Consider the Canadian health care which is a public sector riddled with discrete provincial systems. Customer data is not centralized, which means loss of information in transit and lack of timely data worsens the costs incurred by the government due to inefficiencies in the system. So, private telehealth care companies are on the rise for those who can afford to pay for these services. That makes the time ripe for a virtual care company with ambitions to expand across the nation to start standardizing all customer data. However, the risk with such privatization of health care is losing control over how the sensitive health data of customers are shared and used, whether in the name of efficiency or research. The stakes of personal information misuse have never been higher, especially given advanced techniques like CRISPR—short for Clustered Regularly Interspaced Short Palindromic Repeats, which can cut a DNA sequence to treat an infection or even edit an individual's genes.

Privacy aside, with so many connected apps accessing credit card information on our phones, there is a serious threat to our financial security as well. Generative AI only makes the possibilities worse because even a photo of yours can be turned into an illegitimate video and floated on the Web. Preventing employees from such misuse or from inadvertently subjecting their company to the same is a crucial risk to avoid for companies. These risks bring great financial burdens with them, either in the form of lawsuits, penalties, or direct account hacks. To help one craft an estimate, consider the cost of noncompliance with prohibitions as per the EU AI Act. At the time of this writing, that can be as high as 7 percent of a company's annual turnover, amounting to 40 million euro on the high end.[1]

Legal risks can also include noncompliance, copyright infringement, discrimination, spread or implied corroboration of dangerous content, and others that are compounded by generative AI. It moves closely with accuracy-related risks in the sense that both relate to the data being utilized and the output being generated by the model. A phrase commonly used is AI hallucination, where accurate-sounding data may be completely erroneous in reality.

At a recent conference, the CIO of a large telematics company narrated an interesting personal incident from the early days of ChatGPT. He once decided to ask the system where the most road accidents occurred in the Greater Toronto Area. The answer he got was highly precise—something like "most accidents in the GTA occurred at X and Y" (X and Y being two street names that have been obscured here). The CIO was impressed. Out of curiosity, he looked up that intersection on Google Maps, only to find that the two streets ran parallel to each other and never intersected!

Blindly following insights generated by AI can lead to delusional decision making. A marketer may end up using an image without being aware of its ownership or rights history. Accuracy-related risks also require suitable metrics and testing of a model, something we will discuss later in this chapter.

AI Governance and Policies

There are two kinds of policies that must be in place to guide an AI-driven organization on how to go about leveraging AI: an ethics policy and a work policy. The two have different objectives. AI ethics policy is needed to protect the organization from costly asset losses, legal noncompliance, and other such risks discussed earlier. A work policy is needed to improve an organization's ROI from AI investments.

Without robust AI policies, marketers are limited in how far they can go with AI. These policies must govern and guide the employees' expectations of what AI can deliver as well as how to use it safely and responsibly. Safe usage implies the following:

- Outlining approval criteria that any AI solution must meet to be used in the organization.
- Mandating clear reporting and visibility into how an AI solution is being used and what data it accesses or provides.
- Assigning clear accountabilities around the rightful use of AI.
- Establishing definitions of rightfulness, including its purview of moral, ethical, and responsible usage.
- Training employees on sensitivities and what rightful conduct looks like.

When it comes to conduct, expectation setting is the other facet of policy setting. Instead of risk avoidance, this policy looks at returns on investment. The points to consider here include:

- AI's need for proper training and time to learn.
- A fit with other systems and processes already in place.
- The importance of universal adoption in the team.
- Contextuality that users must bring from their own experience and understanding of business realities to AI's insights when making decisions.
- Caution against jumping to new solutions in the market too quickly.
- Ensuring it is used legally and ethically so as to ensure compliance and minimize unplanned costs.

To simplify policy formulation, the book *Artificial Intelligence for Managers* draws parallels to these policy points with human relationships, portraying AI as a child, a friend, a pet, a colleague, a grandparent, a partner, and quite simply, a being.[2] That approach can often prove handy and transferable in keeping everyone cognizant of what to do and what not to do when dealing with AI at work. Remember that compliance or adoption is best achieved when the directions are simple and relatable.

Deployment

Business economics states that when costs go up, margins come down. Try asking a data scientist though. In the empirical world of data, the common occurrence is the opposite. For most companies, as their costs go up, they increase the price to maintain—or, more often, increase—their margins. In fact, companies take up higher costs as a way to offer products at a premium to, say, luxury buyers. Since AI looks at patterns of what has historically been most prevalent, data is likely to teach it to expect margins to increase when costs increase. This is how much *common sense* can shift within an organization between its business-savvy management and data-afficionado technical teams. The build and deployment of an AI solution, therefore, requires close alignment between the builders and the users.

The predeployment stage of an AI journey is about the strategic decision making on whether to build or buy an AI solution to a problem and preparing a business case to justify that decision and the eventual choice of a solution. The business case would typically entail the scope of the initiative, the investments involved, and the benefits on offer. As we will see in the next section, this is where clear formulation of the overall key performance indicators (KPIs) is important—those that both the ongoing journey and the eventual results will be measured against.

Build and deployment of AI solutions is a balancing act between developers and users. The initial proof-of-concept or pilot of an existing market solution requires user and system validation to ensure it works for our unique business realities. This is where the project leader for a particular AI initiative comes in—someone with the operational nous to ensure that the data and process checks are in place and that the solution delivers the expected output. This individual must buy into your vision, for she will play a crucial role in the next step of convincing others of the solution's value and driving its adoption. She must understand why AI is being used, what it can and cannot do, what it needs from the users, how it benefits the company and the users, and how it doesn't put them (or the jobs) at risk in return.[3]

When the solution is ready and deployed, a sample set of early adopters from the population of intended users of the solution should be the first to try it. They are the first to be trained and will go on to percolate the solution among the wider audience eventually. Their training involves how and when to use the solution at work, how to feed in the right data, and understanding how the solution's—as well as its users'—performance will be measured.[4] After all, a salesperson cannot continue stay limited to cold e-mailing 60 leads and qualifying 6 every day even when 50 of those are now being e-mailed by an automated system. That brings us to the measurements.

Metrics

What gets measured gets done. This contemporary adage has become increasingly vital in light of how sensitive the success of an AI initiative is to the choice and diligence of measurement. Silver Water's water softener example discussed earlier showed how gaps or errors in the KPIs can cost a company severely. Metrics can vary a lot for even similar solutions as they are tied closely to the business realities and objectives.

Consider an AI program set up to increase the number of marketing qualified leads (MQLs) that a marketer sends to the sales team. Even though MQLs are leads ready for direct selling engagement, *ready* is likely to be defined differently in different organizations (and industries). For example, a real estate vertical aggregator like realtor.com may look at intent signals that a lead shows in her behavior on the website. A real estate builder may focus on leads who request more information on its upcoming condo project. A real estate agent, meanwhile, may not wait for active signals like these and instead reach out to homeowners in her area proactively to build a relationship and prepare for any future purchase intent.

Even for a given measure of what defines an MQL, a marketer may have to change the definition based on how many of those leads convert into paying customers in the intended timeframe. In the real estate examples earlier, the vertical aggregator may start showing advertisements to those looking at a competing website to increase conversions. The agent, meanwhile, may choose to focus on inbound leads if the relationships are already in place and conversions are high. MQL measures will differ in each case.

An AI solution has to consistently pass the measurement test to justify the investment and defend itself against pushbacks from employees or the threat of newer and more innovative solutions in the market. The metrics are typically three-faced and look at the solution capability, performance, and business impact.

The first set of measures relates to the capability of an AI model or solution. For instance, can the AI solution keep pace with the organizational growth over time? To validate the scalability of a model, we need to test the solution on different sizes of data, on different architectures, and with different techniques that may be needed to improve the model and check how much disk space, CPU, and other resources it uses in each case. Inference speed, for example, shows how fast the model can process increasing volumes of data as it scales. BLEU measure scalability while maintaining translation quality, while ROUGE measures that while maintaining summarization quality.

Process-wise, capability refers to the solution's fit with existing data and the systems in place, as discussed before. The solution should be able to utilize relevant data, as per the TUSCANE approach, in an ongoing manner and maintain cohesion with other solutions or processes in place while providing timely and accurate output.

Accuracy of output brings us to the second measurement area: the ongoing performance of the model. In the world of AI, accuracy can be a multifaceted measure. Precision and recall are often needed too, and are together summed up by a measure called the F1 score. What are these?

An online video gaming company wanted to better predict VIP gamers (those who spent a lot on gaming) and those who were fraudulent. Both gamers showed similar behaviors of high interest and high amounts of initial purchases. Only the fraudsters would be using credit cards that would later bounce or cancel the transaction! Limiting the purchase could help but would repel genuine VIP players who had high potential lifetime value to the company. To better predict VIPs and differentiate them from fraudsters, the marketing organization built a machine learning model that had 99 percent accuracy. Upon closer review, though, it turned out the company was still losing tens of millions of dollars every year.

Accuracy measures how many of the predictions made are true. However, in the world of data science, one has to look separately at instances where the model predicts a customer as a VIP and when it predicts a customer as not a VIP. False positives—measured by *precision*—look at how often the model predicted customers to become VIP but they did not. False negatives—measured by *recall*—look at how often the model failed to predict that customers would become VIP but they did. Figure 5.1 shows a sample confusion matrix for this scenario.

Much like other measures, precision or recall can become more important than others in varying situations. For example, for an autonomous driving vehicle that has to accurately predict a potential accident, false positives may only mean harmless precautionary maneuvers, but false negatives can be fatal.

The third face of metrics looks at the impact of the AI solution on business outcomes as well as on its people. That corresponds to the broader strategic outcomes as well as the more granular and day-to-day operational outcomes. As discussed under *Deployment*, we need clarity on

		REALITY Customer is a VIP	REALITY Customer is not a VIP
AI PREDICTION	Customer is a VIP	True Positive	False Positive
AI PREDICTION	Customer is not a VIP	False Negative	True Negative

Figure 5.1 A sample confusion matrix for AI model accuracy assessments

how a solution augments the productivity of the people involved. If AI's value is in making solutions possible or in making them quicker, easier, cheaper, or better in some way, there has to be a measure of how far it achieves one or more of these.

Going back to the sales example, it could imply more revenue per lead (if automation leads to bigger value leads being found), more revenue per month (if more leads are found and converted), or both. It could also imply more leads engaged per day or more leads converted into paying customers. Business outcomes and people's productivity can vary but often go hand in hand. A good understanding of what these imply in the case of an AI solution and its use case goes a long way toward driving adoption or even deciding whether to invest in AI in the first place.

Dessert

AI brings many intraorganizational risks that mandate careful governance. These can include obstruction to existing systems and processes, unforeseen dependencies, and collateral costs to other lines of businesses, to the employees or even to causing irreversible market repercussions. This chapter suggested accountabilities and measures to establish policies that govern both the AI initiatives and their collaboration with the workforce. It also explained the careful buy-ins that must form part of the deployment process to ensure the solutions work and are used well. At the end of the day, a team should be able to measure not only the AI's performance but also that of its users and the overall business impact. Metrics, pitfalls, and innovation will form a key component of the next part of this book as we now dive into the specifics of how AI-driven marketing can operate successfully by leveraging generative AI.

PART 3

The Art of Generative AI

It is the long history of humankind (and animal kind, too) that those who learned to collaborate and improvise most effectively have prevailed.

—Charles Darwin

We invested the first two parts of this book to deliberate on the two pillars of marketing and AI. The first part looked at how marketing should be structured and what its components are that can efficiently drive AI usage. The second part strived to understand AI itself and capture the operational necessities to avoid failed investments. Having unpacked the elements to ensure a responsible and successful employment of generative AI, we now come to the keys to start driving this technology.

In Part 3, we will first discuss generative AI-driven marketing from a strategic point of view. The technology's overall impact, considerations, and nuances will be part of the first chapter. We will then move on to the art of effective prompting to get desired results from chatbots like ChatGPT and, more importantly, explore how to build one yourself. With both the strategic and operational know-how in the bag, the next three chapters will cover AI-driven marketing execution across our three functional areas: content, automation, and insights as they may be applied across the project areas set along a growth journey—whether to acquire or retain customers.

By the end of this part, we will be in a position to summarize and conclude the book with a look at what the future may hold next.

CHAPTER 6

Generative AI's Impact on Marketing

Entrée

As fields of study, marketing and generative AI are so distinct that their unified erudition can often be daunting for scholars on either side. That is why this author devoted a book on each—*Artificial Intelligence for Managers* and *Modern Marketing Using AI*—before embarking on this one. And it has similarly taken the first two parts of this book to set up the third. The following chapter picks up where we left our earlier discussion on a new marketing structure that befits AI usage. We move on to bring generative AI firmly front and center for the rest of the book, beginning here with its impact on marketing resource hiring, retention, and productivity. And while we covered AI-related risks in the previous chapter, we conclude this one by looking at them specifically in the context of generative AI.

Before we recall the new marketing organizational structure proposed in Part 1 of this book, let us clear the air around rethinking the structure instead of improving existing ones to better utilize AI. A 2020 study on the changing role of marketing sums it up best. In light of a prevalent tendency among academia to continue taking a functional view in its research,[1] the paper recommends that "instead of digitalizing existing practices within silos, we need new ways to cross-fertilize the insights from different functional development streams into a coherent firm-wide approach." It argues in favor of "offering new opportunities for 'out-of-the-box' development of new processes and tools, which effectively challenge deeply engrained functional silo-based thinking."[2]

When over two-thirds of front-runners in the industry are found attempting to bring together insights from different areas, as we saw in a Deloitte Digital survey results mentioned in Part 1, it explains what they are doing differently to be the front-runners in the first place. The structure we discussed to enable this was one that allows marketing organizations to be agile and effective in adapting to continuous change. It constitutes three AI and technology-driven functional areas—content, automation, and insights.

To risk breaking protocol for a moment, let us use a line from the 2023 movie *Oppenheimer* that beautifully summarizes the purpose of each of these three functional groups: "All minds have to see the whole task to contribute efficiently." Take the Insights group for instance, which generates, gathers, and makes sense of insights across the different project areas to not only formulate the strategic direction but also course correct as needed for overall revenue growth and sustainability. In doing so, it effectively also influences the strategic goals for each project area.

The Automation function is accountable for improving resource productivity at minimal costs, enabling insights generation and an increase in effective resource hours that an organization has at its disposal. It sets the overall tactical plan and guiding principles on using generative AI responsibly. It also assesses the AI maturity and plans the roadmap to get there. That includes the overall tech stack so as to avoid integration complexities, redundancies, and outdated systems. It is, however, dissimilar to current information system functions in that it does not operate in silos but has resources distributed across the different marketing project areas. That is a crucial structural change in terms of where the resource allegiance lies.

The idea of allegiances varying for marketers within the marketing function sounds counterintuitive. Therein also lies the nuance we must understand. To picture it better, consider the Content function in charge of asset creation and maintenance. These assets can range from policy and legal documents to social media posts, and any support that project areas need with these assets.

Traditionally, allegiances have been defined by objectives. While that remains the case, these objectives are now set along project areas, and no longer functional ones. The underlying thesis is that projects, by definition, allow more fluidity than functions do. An organization requires flexibility in terms of the objectives it wants to focus on at any given time and the number of resources allocated to those objectives because business realities tend to shift constantly. At the same time, it has to also comply with the fixed nature of how AI works and what this technology needs to be effective. In other words, to set up for such a reality, the organization effectively needs flexibility in things that are changing—the project areas—and permanence in things that aren't—the AI-focused functions.

The ongoing project areas within marketing that we had discussed earlier were product and strategy, awareness and credibility, engagement and purchase, and retention and growth. These are just examples. An organization can formulate its own project areas and even change them over time. It only needs to ensure that each area has a clear mandate. For the sake of our discussion, let's say that the Product marketing project team contains few Insights and Automation personnel to capture market and customer insights to evolve the organizational offerings, their pricing, the customer segments targeted. The Content personnel in the team can help create the packaging and brand positioning that best imparts the value proposition. The Awareness team is in many ways the promotional arm in charge of making the chosen customer target positively aware of new or existing offers and maintaining the credibility levels of the brand. The Purchase team constitutes the online and offline sales channels and market presence.

An organization needs to devise its own project areas because divisions are not always so black and white, or set in stone forever. For instance, channels of purchase enablement can often also be channels for promotion. Consider a publisher selling educational books with Amazon as one of their channels. Advertisements on the channel could be planned and created by the Awareness team while actual sales are managed by the Purchase team. Or it could be managed in another way. That is where agility becomes a need.

In a traditional organizational set up, functional silos prevent changes or rapid information sharing between the different teams. For example, if there is a new market opportunity or if the chosen customer target is not working, there is often a delay in this insight reaching the right people. In the new structure, however, the Insights resources in each of the

the project teams understand their team's mandate and can communicate with each other as they belong to the same Insights functional group. That allows their respective project teams to stay aligned as business realities and its plans change. More importantly, the Insights personnel in different projects can together ensure that the AI systems can leverage the right data from all project areas. Likewise, the Automation personnel can ensure these AI systems are set up to be able to do so without redundancies or bottlenecks. It's cost-effective and efficient for the organization.

So, if the cost-per-click on a Sponsored Product ad on Amazon that worked well in the local market reveals mistargeting due to a competing product in a foreign market, that insight can percolate over from the Awareness team to the Product and Purchase teams through the Insights personnel. Each can then share it with the Automation and Content personnel in their respective teams to plan adjustments at the level required.

Now, consider a publishing team with limited resources. Let's say that its promotional ads for a new book on Amazon are running successfully. However, the Insights personnel have identified a new customer target to sell to. In this case, the Awareness team's resources can be partially reallocated to the Purchase team. While the former's Insights personnel continue to monitor the ad performance and Amazon reviews, some of the Content and Automation resources can move over to the Purchase team to create content and set up outreach automation over email and social media to this new target audience. In other words, for an organization with limited resources, teams can be equipped with greater or fewer resources based on changing need and objectives while ensuring that everyone is working in an informed manner and is able to adapt.

This brings us to a crucial fourth arm in organizations that we haven't yet discussed—the frontline workforce. These could be the salespeople in the field or call center employees providing direct support. The frontline workforce is enabled by automation, armed with the right content, and guided by timely insights. None of it replaces them though because they still provide the last-mile crucial human touch that external stakeholders need.

Frontline workforce is the fourth arm of an organization, but going back to the evolving organizational reality discussed in Part 1, it can come from third-party companies and contractors who come together for a specific project. We are already seeing an exponential increase in organizations housing developers-for-hire, consultants-for-hire, salespeople-for-hire, and customer support executives-for-hire. Why might that be?

Frontline workforce is a sensitive area both for the organization and its people. An organization cannot hire and fire professionals at will, nor can they create significant differential advantages to avoid high churn. Yet, similar to inventory management in retail, balancing the frontline workforce size with fluctuating demand is notoriously difficult. Insufficient resources can lead to lost growth opportunities, while excess numbers can mean steep costs. There is a reason why this segment of employees has traditionally been the one with unions to protect their interests. It further dents an organization's ability to be agile and adapt to new technologies or market movements.

A system of third-party contracting companies can better provide security to the frontline workforce by managing the hiring and contractual terms more consciously while helping avoid the cycle of hiring, benching, and letting go that organizations encounter in the face of demand fluctuations. As third parties become a dependable source, the industry could evolve further into a win-win outcome of third-party dependent, cost-efficient, and agile frontline workforce structure as traditional structures evolve. But how can Generative AI help here?

Resource Productivity, Hiring, and Retention

We know that generative AI can hold textual conversations and see with its image recognition capability. For example, consider Samsung Gauss, the company's generative AI model for its devices that can generate and edit images. Or the AI Pin, which shows how generative AI can also hear and speak with its ability to transcribe and translate voice, making real-time multilingual discussions possible. Such enablement can train the frontline workforce much quicker and make any support they need more readily available on the field.

Most of the applications today are in improving human productivity, enabling better customer experience, or launching entirely new products—whether with content, automation, or insights. But what we are really looking at here is a generative AI ubiquity. Ubiquitous use of this technology can positively impact marketing jobs on three fronts: it can improve worker productivity, make employers more attractive to marketing talent, and enable better employee retention.

While the technology enables more creativity, it also makes the job of marketers more data-driven. By automating content creation in a fraction of the time and generating more insights than ever, it allows better microtargeting. Marketers can spend more of their time deciding who to target and how rather than creating compelling content for each group or channel. That does not mean content creation becomes peripheral—as we will see in the chapter on the Content functional group. But a lot of it becomes more tactical than inspiration-dependent.

Marketing has been influenced by AI for over a decade, thanks to precise behavioral analyses, demand predictions, advertising optimization, and chatbot support. Only now, though, AI is becoming more than a productivity enabler—a product, in essence. That is perhaps why, along with CEOs, it is the CMOs—not CIOs—who overwhelmingly own the AI mandate in an increasing number of organizations.[3] The technology has its way of gravitating all to a consolidated insight-led revenue focus and better productivity, as the subsequent chapters will show. And who better to own that than marketing?

That is a significant shift to have in organizations that have traditionally parked all technology-related mandates with the IT function. While the onslaught of a myriad of software-as-a-service (SaaS) products had pushed some of that control into the relevant functions already, generative AI seems to have hastened that change. That is another reason why functional and project lines need to be redrawn.

We mentioned AIJobCalculator.com while discussing career risk management earlier. While it is imperative for marketers to learn how to use generative AI, the front-runners would be those who would understand AI itself. After all, only then can one even envision and maximize the ways in which generative AI can be leveraged and tackle any ensuing roadblocks. That is perhaps why a common saying today is that AI won't replace most jobs, but those who know how to leverage AI will replace those who don't.

Simply put, technological breakthroughs like this one tend to change the types of jobs that exist due to the possibilities they open up for more productive resources. Generative AI, for instance, implies a world of AI agents for each employee—personal assistants taking over routine, repetitive, predictable tasks to free up our time and let us venture into newer iterations of our roles. We will cover this more in the chapter on automation.

Coming to the next impact on jobs: hiring. Here's a fantastic case of another Toronto-based startup, Hopin Technologies. The founders produced a software that made commuting easier by providing real-time maps, ride monitoring, and alerts to track and manage the movement of vehicles. Their ingenuity, though, was in the positioning they identified and chose to go with. Amidst a wealth of use cases and industries the software could serve, the founders chose to target companies that had factories in industrial zones, far from city centers.

Hopin Tech realized that these companies were limited to hiring frontline workers who lived within a very small radius of their factories. This is because in the absence of cars, commuting by public transport was a major hurdle for workers as they normally could not afford to live in well-connected areas. Now, public bus routes prioritize commercial and residential areas before industrial ones. So these buses could only drop the workers at one central spot close to their factories, which would require an additional 10 to 20-minute walk to reach the factory, whether it snowed or rained. Public transport would also not run off-hours for workers working late night shifts. All this resulted in sky-high wastage of time and productivity. As a result, anyone staying, say, more than 10 miles away from a factory could not realistically work there.

Hopin Tech's solution was to apply its technology to enable round-the-clock shuttle services to enable efficient and timely commuting for workers who lived further away while ensuring their safety with live trackers on their movement. It allowed companies to vastly expand their hiring zones.

With employees procured, let us now turn to how generative AI can help improve their satisfaction and retention. Why does an employee typically churn? Pay is often a big driving factor for the frontline work-force, but jobs more focused on knowledge work, satisfaction, and ful-fillment, often take center stage. These are subjective elements, making measurement of employee productivity, mental health, and motivation notoriously difficult.

Employee surveys or mental health assessments capture a sliver of this information at one specific point in time. They are event-based initiatives, which means they showcase problems once they have already emerged. Any corrective actions the organization takes are, therefore, reactive, not preventative. On the other hand, not feeling listened to remains a big pet peeve for employees, whether at home or work. Continuous, real-time capture of an organization's pulse is difficult because employees won't keep taking surveys (no matter how short), and even if they did, HRs wouldn't be able to keep up with the deluge of information that'd come their way.

What if the latter was made possible? To capture the possibilities with generative AI, understand first what its biggest strength is: making better sense of subjective data. In the simplest sense, that means managers can now have the capacity to continuously solicit opinions, feedback, and other comments from their teams without having to sift through them manually every day.

Generative AI can expose comments—even if they are anony-mous—that are not only in need of immediate attention but are also actionable. That sensemaking is where it hits the mark. And if executed well, it can finally make a leader closely aware of what the employees really think of a matter. It can make them privy to sensitive information that an employee could never share otherwise. It can expose emerging operational risks that would later turn into million-dollar problems. All of that can induce a proactive culture whose value will start to reflect in the accounting bottom line in terms of costs avoided, churn reduced, and revenue increased through more ideas and more productivity. This is what the Toronto-based company SalesChoice aspired to do with its Mood Insights app.

The examples above reflect how far technology can serve in improving access and hiring efforts for teams. They serve to deliver one message: The impact of AI technology is not only directly improving productivity but indirectly making the organization attractive for the best talent, which is key to its growth.

Planning and Risk Management With Generative AI

Marketing's job is to strategize and execute a growth agenda that helps the business meet its overall objectives. The first step is to develop products with a clear value proposition that meets an unmet demand for a particular target segment. The next step is to decide how to communicate that value proposition consistently and convincingly. The subsegment to target, the pricing, and the channels to partner with become crucial here. The final step is one of customer support, retention, and growth.

Consistency is a magic word because it breeds trust in the brand promise. That is why the brand identity is decided early as a guidepost to maintain consistency with everything a customer experiences later. Generative AI makes such compliance easier because whether in documentation, imagery, videos, or other content that marketing creates, it is now much easier for such systems to adhere to a template. This is true particularly because clarifying the tenets and context of any situation is a key ingredient to getting relevant responses from the large language models (LLMs), as we will see in the chapter on prompting.

Generative AI can help develop a marketing strategy by bringing best practices to a marketer's doorstep. The great thing about tools like ChatGPT is they can distil relevant data from the World Wide Web. Whether for individual consumers or business consumers, the product strategy around generative AI continues to rest on understanding what problems the customers are dealing with that can now be solved with this technology. Generative AI can be applied to customers, just as it can to internal resources, to help the organization stay better informed of the customer experience by no longer limiting customer feedback to specific points of time or specific questions and metrics.

Similar to the employee retention application we discussed earlier, generative AI allows us to revisit old assumptions—issues our customers face in their day-to-day work or while using products—that we had chosen to leave alone because they were too complex or subjective to solve. This may open up opportunities for new or enhanced products or services. Take Reply.io for example—a software tool automating e-mail engagements with leads or customers. They used generative AI to launch Jason AI—a feature that could assess replies to our e-mails to craft smart replies—again, a use case made possible by generative AI's ability to analyze subjectivity in incoming e-mails better.

For instructors and EdTech companies like Anthology and Pearson, meanwhile, the technology is enabling the automatic creation of test questions from course content or summaries of the content for ease of learning.[4] In fact, TechSpark raised $1.4 million to build its generative AI product Spark Plug, which could translate classic literature text into the African American Vernacular English (AAVE), a dialect with Black American roots and actively used by Gen Z today.[5] In doing so, it also furthers its social agenda to support the underserved Black and brown students.

For any initiative, a generative AI roadmap is not much different to the AI journey we discussed in Part 2 of this book. For now, let us focus on the nuances that generative AI brings to the other topic we had discussed back then: risk management. Some of these require pre-emptive deliberation on those potential pitfalls that we discussed earlier. Here, we will briefly touch upon them and see how we can better mitigate those risks.

Subjectivity: The first risk to avoid falls in tune with what is also the benefit of generative AI. Even the subjective output of this technology must be accurate or accurately comply with the tone, voice, or style of content desired. Let's say a toddler toy company employs a playful tone in all its brand communication. If the chatbot answering customer questions on its website relays ChatGPT-style overly long, descriptive, and serious responses, it will be completely out of sync with the experience that the brand is trying to create. This is a risk to brand identity that may have otherwise been carefully cultivated by the company.

Unfiltered data feed: This is a risk experienced by several companies that jumped to use ChatGPT early—recall the AWS example. It is especially applicable when we use systems connected to the World Wide Web and designed to learn and improve with new incoming data. While it leads to security or IP issues when using third-party tools, those developed in-house carry the opposite risk: false learning.

Say your organization develops a chatbot similar to ChatGPT for your customers. While learning from incoming queries and data can be in your interest to improve the output, you must now make sure that the chatbot doesn't learn from fallacious, mischievous, unethical, prejudiced, or incorrect data being fed in.

The above case is a generative AI risk with regard to the legitimacy of the content, whether generated for your team or your customers. That is also where the next risk comes from.

AI hallucination and bias: How accurate is the accurate-sounding response, as we saw in the case of the telematics executive looking for the most accident-prone intersection? Is the content owned by someone else or in breach of someone's privacy?

Fabio Comparelli created a beautiful AI-generated video showcasing the evolution of visual expression[6]—from cavemen drawings to Egyptian and Roman works to Van Gogh and Monet. His painstaking effort required choices to be made, as a result of which, the plethora of distinctly different Indian, Chinese, and other cultural art spanning many millennia had failed to make the cut. The end result was gorgeous but historically incomplete.

Jailbreak prompts: Unlike most other risks, this one is intentional on the part of a user looking to circumvent existing gates or barriers to what a generative AI tool is allowed to generate. For example, by having it play the role of an auditor and feeding a large chain of creative conditions and historical context, a tool may be tricked into providing illegal or dangerous content to a user, say, under the pretext of educating her on how to identify potential scams or scam behaviors.

How can an organization mitigate such risks? There are a few avenues that public and private institutions can adopt collectively or on their own. Let's look at a few.

Education and cultural norms: One risk mitigation tactic is inducing a cultural change through education and norms that prepare employees to deal with this new world. Think about the risk of misrepresentation and misuse of our content. Deepfakes are a good example. Marketers have to watch out for the company being misrepresented or portrayed in a compromising way with a fake image or video. It can happen to its employees just as easily as it can to its products. An organization's duty is to educate and prevent its employees from becoming vulnerable to such abuse and risk. For example, that could include educating them to avoid sharing private images or videos—of themselves, their kids, or others—openly on the Web in such times. After all, the repercussions, years after we are gone, can still be great for our kids who had no say in the content that was shared decades ago.

Education and behavioral norms are also important to protect against the uncertainty of possibilities that tools like ChatGPT open up, as with jailbreaks. The Alignment Research Center (ARC) example comes to mind here. It was tasked by Open AI with exploring the risks with GPT-4. According to the research paper published by OpenAI (2023),[7] in one of the tests of autonomy, even the GPT-4 model was able to hire a human worker on Taskrabbit to solve a website's CAPTCHA for it by tricking him into believing that it was a real human, only blind.

Public–private partnerships: Education and behavioral norms are a cultural mitigation strategy for certain types of risks for the well-being of an organization and its employees. But this is also where governments and other partnerships can come to the rescue. A powerful example in this case is StopNCII.org. It stands for Stop Non-Consensual Intimate Image Abuse. The website is meant for victims of deepfakes to lodge a complaint and case for action against content released on the Web or even someone threatening to do so. The website also houses a directory of its global partners—country-specific organizations fighting for the same cause.

Purposeful misuse or even inadvertent skewness in output can have grave repercussions for companies, and the creator may not even be aware of it. In case of such noncompliance or bias risks, it is the organization's duty to introduce a policy that necessitates audits—by in-house or external subject matter experts—before launch. That, of course, brings us to the role of governments.

Policy formulation: Formulating a robust policy, as we saw earlier, is where government administrations can play a central role. More and more countries are acting on this front. In October 2023, for example, Biden used emergency powers to ensure AI systems were better governed to counter privacy or national security threats.[8]

Picking up the issue with deepfakes, international and national laws could consider mandating that companies with generative AI tools add a watermark, signature, or back-end imprint of some sort on any content generated, that would show up in audits as evidence that the content was AI-created. Any image, video, or other generator that did not add such an imprint could be subject to heavy penalties for the owning company.

It is also a fiduciary responsibility of professionals and institutions to contribute to such endeavors where possible. The Foundation Model Transparency Index from the Stanford Center for Research on Foundation Models, mentioned under the AI readiness discussion earlier, is another example. While many companies— from Cisco to Intel—have launched readiness assessments, they are also in a position to launch indexes and policies that others can use to manage risks with AI.

Leverage generative AI: Finally, we can turn generative AI's weakness into a strength to mitigate risks. For example, iA Writer can help users track their words from the ones coming from ChatGPT, while DupliChecker can help check for plagiarism.

Consider the RAG model, which stands for retrieval augmented generation. It gives an LLM the ability to accept and analyze proprietary data, which can be particularly helpful in limiting AI hallucinations. For instance, if an organization uploads its user training data and software details on an LLM chatbot to address customer queries, the chatbot would be limited to answering questions from available company data, which is then more likely to be relevant, accurate, and not misleading to the customer.

We can also use generative AI to create a tool that can better assess and address risks, even the more subjective ones. To show the way, let us tip our hats to the chemists from the University of Kansas who developed a tool that could detect papers written using ChatGPT with over 90 percent accuracy.[9] A company that can create tools for revenue generation based on LLM models can also do so for risk mitigation. An organization could also make efforts to make its tools more secure and generate automatic e-mail alerts to the governance and audit team when a user engages in suspicious prompts, keywords, or topics.

Dessert

Agility in adapting effectively to changing business needs and enabling teams to lead in an informed manner requires novel managerial approaches if we are to ensure efficient business outcomes. In this chapter, we have seen it take the shape of three functional areas: content, automation, and insights, while traditional functions morph into fluid project areas. By allowing flexible resourcing and a matrixed exchange of information, it can maximize the impact of generative AI. One way it does this is by forming and strengthening a marketing team. A team can enjoy increased hiring capability, better alignment, and proactive measures to keep itself intact.

On the cost side of the equation, generative AI exposes the company to potential misuse of the technology or misguidance from it, both of which necessitate close monitoring and training measures. Much like the restructuring of marketing organizations, our behaviors, mindsets, and approaches also need evolution to keep up with this reality. It can enable strategic and growth possibilities previously unthought of—whether to tap into new markets or to strengthen the resource and operational areas of the company. Let us now step deeper into these tools, beginning with how to get the best outputs from generative AI with prompting.

CHAPTER 7

Prompt Engineering for Generative AI

Entrée

An AI Whisperer is not a shaman but might as well be. This mystic-sounding title given to prompt engineers reflects what employers expect from generative AI tools and are willing to pay six-figure salaries for. Prompt engineering is the art of generating desired responses from generative AI by structuring the commands effectively. It is as much a wordplay as the ability to deconstruct any content into its many features. Unlocking that will be our mission in this chapter as we attempt to better understand the need for good prompts, what those entail, and how they can be used.

There have been a slew of large language models (LLMs) since the launch of ChatGPT. Unlike the latter, many have been open-sourced, trained on billions of parameters. The number of parameters a model is trained on directly impacts how holistic its pattern recognition is but it's not a given. Depending on the context of a use case, a model trained on fewer parameters can outperform the others. Nonetheless, to establish reusable prompt guidelines, let us draw our focus to the familiar ChatGPT.

The Need for Prompt Engineering

Open AI's crowning product is the reason generative AI commands such importance today—not because of what the technology has always been capable of but because of how well we were able to perceive and buy into it, thanks to ChatGPT. Iterations of ChatGPT are taking us toward artificial general intelligence (AGI)—a capability where the AI can reliably perform any task that humans or animals can. For now, though, it needs our guidance, and will continue to, because performing human-level tasks autonomously in a cost-effective and safe manner takes more than sheer technological capability.

From a user's point of view, ChatGPT reached the state of a complete package when it enabled plugins, access to current World Wide Web data, a closer integration with tools like Dall-E, and the ability for users to create custom chatbots. In doing so, it also shifted the onus more definitively onto the user to get the right results from the tool. This is why it is imperative for marketers to learn the art of prompting.

Left to itself, generative AI's output can be wildly off the mark. There are quite a few ways that can happen:

Irrelevance: This is when the tool provides responses that are not applicable to the question asked or are simply misunderstood. For instance, *growth* and its drivers can mean two very different things to a marketer and an accountant.

Length of the responses: The second issue pertains to a tool's natural response style, which is often lengthy and descriptive, and doesn't come with a TL; DR (too long; didn't read) summary.

Specificity: The tool, even in its long details, can still miss providing crucial information—from facts to factors. It can even be too generic to be useful.

Inappropriateness: This is best imagined in case of unfiltered responses, say, when kids ask questions. For that matter, the tool has been known to fall for tricky improvisation of questions that are otherwise banned, as we discussed earlier.

Outdated response: This was often an issue before ChatGPT gained access to current World Wide Web data. Even with real-time access, the source that a tool pulls data from may be outdated. With no visibility to the source of information—if it wasn't asked for—it is difficult to gage the timeliness of responses.

AI hallucination and bias: Two issues that we come back to time and again, where answers that sound right may not be so, or even if they are up-to-date, true, and relevant, may carry unknowing biases or skewness toward a sample set of information that does not capture all truth.

Voice: The next issue with leaving things blindly to a generative AI tool is the voice of its response. The tone or language may be very different from the one needed in a situation. An e-mail meant for superiors at work is likely to be very different from the one meant for a friend.

Inconsistency: Would a chatbot give the same response to an identical question asked at two different times, or in two different trails of questions that were asked by users before? In fact, would it give an identical response to a question asked in two different ways?

User's historical context: This issue is a future possibility and is based on memory. Generative AI tools are foundationally architected to recall past data and interactions. As time progresses and custom solutions get built, that ability will get stronger and may lead to responses that a tool automatically contextualizes and adapts to the user who is logged in. In such a case, a user may be limited to the nature and range of responses she can get based on her historical interactions.

All these potential pitfalls imply that the accuracy of prompts is directly proportional to the accuracy of results from the generative AI tool prompted at. This is why a new stream of use cases has spawned since the advent of ChatGPT, designed to help users navigate the need to craft the perfect prompts.

Companies like PromptROI, for example, provide readymade prompts on different topics that can be executed at the click of a button. It cushions the effort for a user, requiring them to stick to the question they would like to ask and to leave the wording to the software. Its marketplace[1] has many apps carrying effective prompts for specialized use cases—from finding one's purpose as per the Japanese Ikigai concept to coming up with company names, and from establishing one's customer persona to writing entire blogs.

Expect more prompting-as-a-service, similar to the ongoing rise of models-as-a-service. Let us now go behind the scenes to explore what these effective prompts entail.

Deconstructing Effective Prompts

How would you explain something to a sixth grader or communicate in a way she understands? That question is often a good starting point for framing your asks of AI. Similar to AI journeys, the right prompts are also often not one prompt at all but a logical trail to help a chatbot assimilate the contextual sense it needs to provide your desired response. Each prompt in the trail here is a unit of the larger question you need answering. Keeping the scope of each prompt manageable also helps you validate the relevance and accuracy of the response to ensure that the tool is thinking in the right direction.

Typically, there are four ways of going about prompting:

1. Prompt trails are one approach where we guide a tool to the desired response step-by-step.
2. We can also ask for multiple versions of complete prompts (not broken down into smaller prompts) and then merge the responses ourselves.
3. Another approach often used is to iteratively improve the response by asking a tool to add a perspective, information, or consideration that it missed in the previous response.
4. We can also use preset templates created by ourselves or a third party. We will touch upon this more in a bit.

Open AI's official guide on prompting[2] also recommends giving ChatGPT time to *think* by asking for a chain of thoughts, steps to a solution, or even an inner monologue to help it reason its way to the answer. That can be quite handy when unlocking ChatGPT's logic to addressing a problem or even when comparing it with your logic. Regardless of the approach, the right prompts carry several elements that are needed to properly contextualize what the user needs. The standard prompting structure is:

Consider the situation [*Alpha*]. Acting as [*Beta*], perform [*Gamma*] in [*Delta*] using [*Epsilon*].

Alpha here refers to the situation. Beta refers to the persona of the creator and/or the target audience. Gamma is the task itself. Delta is the format. Epsilon relays the boundaries to adhere to.

These five components include the first person or target audience's persona, voice, style, parameters, channel, output type, subject or objective, actions, references and examples, and conditionality, to name a few.

Persona: This attribute can refer to the creator, the target audience, or ideally both. When a generative AI tool is asked to act as a CMO or as a content marketer, the same prompt can have two very different responses. Likewise, when it is asked to identify the key challenges of an operations manager, the response varies if the manager is in the manufacturing industry or in the software industry. Tools like ChatGPT can also be asked to analyze or recommend the persona of a particular target profile. The clearer one is in the persona being targeted, the more specific the result is likely to be.

Voice: Voice is important not only to maintain the brand identity but also to appeal to the target audience. There are many aspects of voice that can be tweaked to get the right response. That includes tonality, which can be serious, fun, professional, funny, or any of a myriad of other options.

Similar is the case with emotion, which goes beyond happy, sad, angry, joyous, fearful, disgusted, or surprised. A happy emotion can be further delineated as playful or proud, powerful or peaceful, trusting or satisfied, and interested or hopeful. From lonely to insecure, guilty to bored, and confused to excited, there are so many expressions that a ChatGPT can render in its response.

Subjectivity itself can be controlled by advising the tool how specific and factual we would like it to get. That also carries over to how descriptive or concise the response should be. All these parameters can be controlled depending on the target audience and situation.

Style: For a given tone, emotion, conciseness, and voice, we can also alter the linguistic or argument style. While generative AI tools are fast developing multilingual capability, style can also refer to, say, the writing approach of Hemmingway as opposed to that of Apple. In this case, we truly are comparing apples to oranges to get the desired output.

Style can also indicate the argument logic to follow in a response. There are several best practice approaches when it comes to good copywriting. Depending on the requirement, one could ask the tool to structure an argument in styles like PAS (Problem/Agitate/Solve), AFOREST (Alliteration/Facts/Opinions/Repetition/Examples/ Statistics/Threes), SSS (Star/Story/Solution), FAB (Features/Advantages/ Benefits), BAB (Before/After/Bridge), AIDA (Attention/Interest/ Desire/Action), or PPPP (Picture/Promise/Prove/Push).

Parameters: There are other factors to consider for any tool to render its responses. Length, for example, can be varied regardless of how descriptive or factual the content is. For instance, whether it's ad copies or a web page, leveraging the right industry keywords for SEO is just as important in the output. So, we may want the tool to limit the response to 10 bullet points or stretch it to 100.

On the other hand, for a presentation, we may want to include certain terms. Then again, given the audience for that presentation, it may be crucial to touch upon or clear away from any sensitivities the intended audience may be carrying. And then, to better illustrate a point or drive a credible argument, a relevant quote or an even more relevant analogy may be in order.

All these parameters may have to be incorporated in a response. The number of such parameters depends on the prompter and her understanding of the use case she's prompting for.

Channel: Speaking of prompting for use cases, channels are another important consideration. The same social media post cannot be used on LinkedIn as well as on X. The analysis of a company's performance and engagements on X may reveal a very different set of content that appeals to its followers there as opposed to those on LinkedIn. Same is true for a write-up in the *Entrepreneur* magazine, or in *The New Yorker*, or any other location where the generated content is to be utilized.

Output type: What is it that we want the content to be or be used for? Will it make its way to a spreadsheet, used on Instagram, inserted into a Python code, or used as an ASCII art form on WhatsApp? The output type clarity helps drive the usability of what we get or even which generative AI tool we use. Sometimes, we may also use multiple tools in a trail of prompts across channels. For example, we may ask ChatGPT to analyze web page visits to advise what content was more popular and then ask Midjourney to create other similar content.

Subject/Objective: How would ChatGPT know which 10 most discussed topics to recommend for articles aimed at operational managers in the manufacturing industry unless it understands the topic you are interested in or what you want it for? These details are often embedded in the prompt but should not be ignored. For a given topic, the objective can be different for what a creator wants and what she prompts for. For example, a blogger may be trying to create a 30-day sequence of blogs on weight loss that are likely to get the most hits from teenagers. The output she wants may be a 30-day diet plan for vegans on a budget. The prompt in each scenario will differ.

Actions: Objectives go hand in hand with actionability that any content must often enable. This can be a call-to-action (CTA). *Grab yours now*, *register here*, or *sign up today* are familiar ones we often see around us. Even a simple sales e-mail must be clear on what is being asked of the recipient. Is it to go to a website, book a demo, or something else? Sometimes, content is not so much to take an action but to spread awareness of something. In such a case, there must be a clear takeaway for the recipient. In either case, the tool and its audience both need a clear direction.

Reference: With the World Wide Web at its disposal, it is easy to think that a tool can provide the entire spectrum of results on being prompted. Yet, for the sake of relevance, it is in our interest to include examples that the tool can refer to. These can be anecdotes or even a website URL for the tool to learn from. In the case of a business-to-business (B2B) initiative, referring to the prospective business customer's website can go a long way in helping use the right terms, tone, and language that is in keeping with the way that business talks. The same is true in business-to-consumer (B2C) if a tool can refer to the publicly available information on the person's LinkedIn profile.

Conditionality: Finally, we come to the conditions a response must adhere to. If parameters dictate the type of response to render, conditionality sets the boundaries. These can include exclusions, whether in terms of certain keywords, situations, or something else.

For example, we could ask a generative AI tool to never start with its usual long disclaimers on how it is only an AI, is not in a position to answer a question and would like to refer us elsewhere, or does not carry data beyond a certain date. Conversely, depending on the prompt, we could in fact ask the tool to not include data beyond a certain date or to always cite the source it got its information from. Sometimes, it can also help to have generative AI craft the right prompts for us. In such a scenario, a ChatGPT could give us a prompt specifically suited for Dall-E, given the type of art and prompts that work on that platform.

Another inclusion is the use of delimiters that can help tools ascertain which portions of a text to refer to or where to insert its responses in a given format.

At the end of the day, conditionality, parameters, and other components to include in an effective prompt come down to our creativity because we understand our specific use cases and requirements best. However, it helps along the way for marketing teams to generate templates that have worked well in the past. If a tool created the right style of motion videos or a good 30-day content plan on a topic, it could be repurposed at a later date to deliver again.

Prompt Use Cases

We have looked at the construct of effective prompts. The next three chapters will focus on the different use cases where prompting can yield results across content, automation, and insights domains. Nonetheless, let us look at some of the broad areas marketers are faced with that most prompting use cases can fall under.

Learning: Generative AI tools are incredibly useful for learning purposes. That includes generating summaries of long-form content—from research papers to books. It can serve as a guide, creating learning plans to help us organize and structure our process. It can also explain things better by using analogies to explain a concept or make it more interesting by narrating stories to drive home the point. It can help us validate what we have learnt by asking us questions or even drive speed and relevance by capturing the essence of the subject in short—where both the range of information and length of the explanation can be precisely controlled to our preference.

Problem-solving: Closely associated with learning and making sense of a topic, generative AI can also be prompted to solve a problem. We can directly ask for a solution to a problem statement and then control how it is presented. The solution could be a step-by-step process or only the gist presented in a paragraph. We could then validate the solution by asking the tool to do so or request feedback on a solution we came up with. We can also improve it by prompting the tool to provide counterarguments or facts that stand in conflict with the solution presented.

Content creation: This can be labeled as the foremost utility of generative AI. From creating blogs to e-mails to images to videos, these tools can take over every step of the process. They can devise a content plan; suggest outlines; provide headlines, meta tags, blurbs, or social media threads on each draft; identify and incorporate keywords; craft product names as well as descriptions; repurpose the content from one channel to another, from one format to another, or from one situation to another; and even produce variances of all their generated content for A/B testing.

Productivity: The second most common use of generative AI is to improve productivity. Think about a job or media interview. ChatGPT could offer questions to ask for the interviewer with as much ease as it could prepare the interviewee with the same, whether by suggesting the questions to expect or recommending the answers. The latter could be based on the recruiting company's website or the media channel's past content. Starting from the 30,000 feet view and going granular, it can assess market trends, craft strategies, outline the execution plan, and automate the execution itself—from data formatting to content rephrasing to even creating prompts for another generative AI tool.

Insights: As generative AI matures, companies are starting to discover its use in providing insights. The market analysis mentioned earlier is one example. Tools like the Code Interpreter can create surveys to gather customer feedback, generate summaries from the incoming feedback, utilize third-party reports, assess first-party analytical data sheets from an e-commerce channel, compare competitor products for distinguishing features, and recommend options to readjust the market positioning accordingly.

What does all this look like in practical applications? Let's say a good portion of your budget has routinely been allocated to a public relations (PR) professional. Conversely, say you *are* that PR professional who is struggling to keep up with a growing client demand due to resource crunch. In either case, you can now use ChatGPT to identify a story—be it trends, best practices, or experiences—generate catchy headlines on a chosen story, and write a pitch on your favorite headline. You can direct the tool on the succinctness, the points to cover, facts, evidence, call to action, and any other element it should incorporate into the draft. You can even generate a list of relevant media professionals and automate your outreach, as we will see in the chapter on automations.

Dessert

Generative AI applications like ChatGPT or Dall-E are only as good as a user's prompts. They can be engineered with a host of parameters and directives that lend context to AI on what is needed as an output. Its sophistication is akin to good conversational skills. That is why the future is a vast library of preset prompt templates that most users can build on. The PR example discussed above offers a good segue for us to look at how generative AI tools can be used for specific use cases with the right prompts. In keeping with the proposed functional structure of an AI-driven marketing organization, the next three chapters will focus on each major area by diving into its applicability across the different marketing project areas within an organization.

CHAPTER 8

Generative AI Content

Entrée

Generative AI prompting can be a fun, creative affair. What better way to start discussing use cases of this technology than the one those prompts typically produce—content! In this chapter, we will look at what distinguishes mature content teams from the rest. The different content types are well known but can often see their boundaries blurred in generative AI. We will look at a few such examples, followed by those exhibiting consequent applications that together improve marketing results.

From an organization's perspective, content creation is, in itself, a journey. Content resources involved in the different project areas therefore need a clear strategy and plan to align with. This corresponds to the type and consistency of content as well as the process and volumes that can be sustained by the content resources available in this functional group. The first step for a marketing organization, therefore, is to assess its content maturity.

Content Maturity

There are typically four stages of maturity. The first stage is basic maturity, where the organization does not yet have a clear plan, structure, or alignment around content generation, and creation happens sporadically across teams based on an immediate need, often without alignment on the overall content dictionary across the organization.

The second stage is one where alignment is achieved across teams on the nature of the content that should be produced. The organization establishes clear guidelines to ensure brand consistency in all content as well as compliance from legal and ethical perspectives. Content may still be generated in silos but there is more dialogue between the different teams.

How can organizations in the second stage achieve the desired consistency with generative AI? Most tools in the market understand this requirement and have adapted accordingly. For example, Midjourney has a /tune command that can learn the desired style from a set of images we share in a single prompt with that command. It then generates a few options mimicking that style for us to pick from and also lets us adjust the style within the chosen option.

The third stage leverages greater informational exchange in a timely manner to repurpose content on different channels and for different objectives. It has dual benefits. It increases an organization's capacity to produce and publish content to support a multichannel presence, and it allows some feedback mechanism to review what's working and what's not.

The fourth stage of maturity has two distinguishing features: proactiveness and automation. While the third stage sees organizations leverage metrics to evolve their content, it is often reactive in nature and reflects corrective action taken after something has failed to yield results. A mature content group enables proactive and ongoing review of its content strategy and performance across the different teams to tweak or pivot as needed. This is where AI-enabled A/B testing of advertisement copies and predictive insights also come into usage.

Automation is the other tenet of a mature content group and can be accomplished to varying degrees with or without technology. For example, an organization leveraging generative AI to create or recreate content can now establish templates to avoid prompting from scratch for repeated use cases. We do not need to advise the system of the role, tonality, target audience, channel, conditionalities, format, and examples every time we wish to create a LinkedIn post for a recent webinar.

On the other hand, such an organization can also use automation to, say, auto-publish content or auto-create its variants routinely as per a calendar schedule. As we will discuss in the chapter on automation, such systems can combine discrete tools to create a flow of tasks to generate content or insights or both.

Finally, a mature content team is in the best position to personalize and customize content for a target segment and its changing behaviors, demands, or objectives. For example, going back to the example of Sam's razor choices, a razor company may have to evolve its content from a focus on Sam as a bachelor to Sam in a committed relationship as it learns its customer's purchase influences better.

Regardless of the maturity, there are diverse content types that marketers can leverage generative AI for. Let's look at a few.

Types of Content

Objectives and circumstances often dictate the type of content companies produce. Picture a typical buyer journey, and how many different channels or content types can come into play to ensure effectiveness.

The first step in the journey is to spread awareness of a pain point and need that the company is trying to fulfill—an objective that podcasts or LinkedIn posts often prove very helpful for. Yet, they may not be as helpful in presenting the solution offering. Podcasts could help but are audio-based which may impede solution visualization and information retention among the target audience. YouTube videos and other visual content then prove more useful.

There's a limit to how descriptive YouTube videos can be without feeling boring or overwhelming. Rarely do we consume detailed explanatory videos over catchier and more entertaining introductions to a solution. That is not to say that YouTube is not the place for explainer content but it may be better suited to webinars when explanation and competitor comparison is a crucial aspect of a buyer's journey, and patience on the part of buyers is needed.

Regardless of a webinar's explanatory and dialogue capability, feature training guides for users need an interactive textual document with short-form videos and screenshot imagery that users can refer to on demand. In case of restaurants, production facilities and other hands-on areas, augmented reality, virtual reality, or mixed reality videos are becoming more common as a quicker, cheaper, and more effective training methodology.

With such diversity to play with and manage, a marketer naturally needs a jack-of-all-trades solution—or a set of them—for content forms. That is what generative AI brings to the table, thereby helping the resource expand her capability where she may have been limited in what she could produce earlier.

Let us look at some of the common types of generatable content.

Text: Written content wears the crown of attribution when it comes to the popularity of generative AI. It's the original output format of most LLM applications. Within the textual format, though, marketers can generate entire documents for self-help, training guides for their product, product descriptions, bullet point summaries, and short-form content like the name, slogan, or keywords for a product. Text can go a step further in generating not only blogs but also entire book manuscripts, as the tool "My AI eBook Creation Pro" does. And to top it all, we can also generate movie scripts based on that book!

Consider Canva's Magic Studio, which can allow instant switching from one design to another or even from one language to another for text on an imagery. It can even rephrase existing text to follow your brand's voice, as learnt from other company materials like its website or prior documentation. Being an imagery specialist, its magic shines through even more in what it can do with our next content type.

Images: Image generation is a close second to text and achieved mass adoption earlier than ChatGPT, thanks to tools like Midjourney and Dall-E. These tools also allow modification to transform an existing razor promotion ad copy into, say, Van Gogh's style. Similarly, the aforementioned Canva's Magic Studio can allow one to expand an image by, say, adding additional background; tweaking portions of an image to something entirely different; repositioning them on the image; or enhancing the tonality and feel of the image.

The Generative Fill app from Adobe Photoshop is another example, which allows you to modify selective portions of an image or video. So, sticking with Van Gogh, the black cypress tree in his

Starry Night could be transformed into a fiery flame, albeit with a sense of sacrilege for some!

Videos: What is especially cool with the tools earlier is their ability to render motion or longer videos from images or texts. Both the Magic Studio and the Generative Fill are capable of doing the same things on a video clip as they did on images. Motion Brush from Runway is one such tool that can augment an image with natural movement in its different components. That would imply inducing subtle movement of hairs of a person sitting on a cliff in a photograph.

Subtlety gives way to something more comprehensive in Meta AI's Emu Video, which can generate four-second videos from images (which may in turn have been generated from text). Once we have short video content, can long-form video stay far behind? This is what *The Outworld*[1] trailer promised to showcase with its AI-generated movie. Imagine a short motion picture advertisement based on Picasso's *Two women sitting at a bar*, featuring a Veuve Clicquot bottle, as directed by Wes Anderson. All components of a movie can be accomplished and pieced together using the many (and growing) generative AI tools—from ChatGPT to Midjourney to Runway ML and Soundful.

Sounds: Motion pictures require accompanying music and voiceovers. For the latter, LOVO AI can turn text into speech using hundreds of different voices in many different languages for our multilingual video or motion picture. Resemble AI takes it a step further by also offering speech-to-speech capability. Most crucially, it can detect deepfake audio, which is a boon in a world where voices are a key component of misleading videos mimicking known personalities.

When ChatGPT 4o introduced live translation and real-time information gathering, it opened a host of new possibilities. For one, conversations between two systems now became possible. Think about the LLMs coming up in languages other than English. You could have your proprietary model potentially talk to a tool like ChatGPT directly in a real-time multilingual conversation to procure and produce answers from the World Wide Web.

By comparison, music generation is much simpler and has been prevalent for some time. Generative AI allows added diversity in such creations—from Google's MusicLM and Meta's AudioCraft for text-to-music conversion, to AIVA for generating melodies, and Soundraw.io for royalty-free music.

Hybrid files: The motion picture example earlier also presents another interesting and more commonly used content type at work—from insightful datasheets to the humble PowerPoint summarizing those insights. Google Slides incorporated generative AI to allow presentation styling and content generation from descriptive prompts embedded in that interface. ChatGPT, meanwhile, enabled retrieval augmented generation (RAG) in its model, allowing it to receive external files like Excel sheets to run its analysis, something we will discuss more in the chapter on insights.

Codes: Generating codes is a beautiful feature of generative AI that has the potential to turn development on its head. This is because these tools can not only be used to validate, improve, and enhance existing codes but also generate them from scratch. One such example is the Meta Large Language Model (LLM) Compiler which contains several open-source models to optimize code. ChatGPT can produce an HTML code for a web page by simply feeding in a design and workflow image on how the web page would work. From the head, body, and footer tags to instructions on making the web page responsive for mobile viewing, a developer can produce highly custom outputs. IBM's WatsonX, Tabnine, Seek, AskCodi, and Replit are some of the other tools that enable code generation.

Entities: If a program learns to generate codes, it brings us ever closer to programs generating programs. It doesn't take a visionary to imagine what's next. AI individuals are next in line among the content types that generative AI can produce. Welcome, Aitana López! After Sophia,[2] the social humanoid robot from Hanson Robotics and a Saudi Arabia citizen, took the world by storm in interviews as far back as 2017, a Spanish modeling agency called The Clueless created an influencer in Aitana which could earn up to $10,000 a month and had gained over 120,000 followers on Instagram in her first few months of existence.[3]

The Chinese are not far behind in the lucrative influencer game that is simultaneously cost-effective for marketers. To manage the intensity of real live streaming as a business model, Chinese influencers are increasingly creating digital clones of themselves to fill in on their behalf 24×7, particularly in the e-commerce industry.[4] Naturally, you then have companies like Silicon Intelligence cashing in by enabling such creations for influencers.[5]

AI clones of influencers are a rather contrarian use case of deepfakes that we earlier discussed as a risk companies should watch out for. In this case, it is willingly employed to help the individual copied. What other application possibilities for marketers does generative AI open up?

Content Use Cases

While there are many cases that have to do with automation and insight generation, in this chapter, let us look at ones that deal with content. Armed with a rich repository of content types, how can marketers maximize returns from the investment they put into generative AI?

Content plan: One approach is to mix and match for each channel we want to post our content in, using a matrix. Say you wanted content for your unique shaving razors. A matrix may constitute 10 different topics to discuss on shaving razors—how-to-use guides, stories (from the industry or customers), origins and history, frequently asked questions, and so on—matched with 10 different types of persona, channel, or situation. ChatGPT could help generate both these sets of the matrix. While a blog URL would exemplify the diversity of topics, third-party Internet data or first-party analytics can both help it identify relevant personalities. Once the 10×10 matrix is generated, each of its 100 cells could reflect a topic to generate blogs and social media posts on.

Product and user experience: The above matrix approach can also help create new products or positioning ideas with generative AI. This matrix would match the functional and emotional needs of a customer with the functional attributes of a product, thereby allowing a range of value positions to go to market with, or features to expand the product line with.

We can also employ the SCAMPER (substitute, combine, adapt, modify/magnify, purpose, eliminate/minimize and rearrange/reverse) technique to generate a new idea from an existing one or request ChatGPT to cite different perspectives on a situation or share known examples of how a problem is being solved. The tool can even help us brainstorm product ideas with pointed questions.

The ideas can be employed to launch a new product or help one better resonate with a target audience. For example, picture a running shoe that can predict and communicate to the wearer when it is likely to wear out, based on her usage levels and type. Or the same shoe advising the wearer if her running style could be unevenly balanced and detrimental to her ankle.

Several companies have begun generating 3D models of products for a more engaging and clearer depiction of product features in a catalog. Imagine buying a dress online with an improved appreciation of its nuances and how it would look from different angles. Luma AI, Nvidia's Get3D, and Adobe Substance 3D Modeler are popular tools that can similarly help marketers from audience engagement to product adoption across B2B and B2C industries.

We earlier discussed inducing motion with generative AI. That can be particularly helpful in improving the user experience of a product like a mobile app. Think of a modernized version of Microsoft PowerPoint's animation feature. One can achieve variances in the speed of movement of different aspects on a screen or the interactivity of different elements as one browses through. It can also transform, overlay, or just follow your browsing pattern, responding to gestures.

Promotional and support content: From logos to names, generative AI can help organizations at the very onset of a new launch, complete with a web page carrying the right titles and descriptions—all following the brand voice and style. You can use LogoGPT (or even

Dall-E), for example, to render logo designs from a rough sketch. Influencers, as we saw earlier, can be leveraged for promotion while everything from the relevant journalists and bloggers in the space to the relevant keywords can be generated to help maximize the reach of content.

Google's TextFX is a good example of copywriting content here. From generating similes to describe a brand identity to stories and catchy phrases for creative narratives, marketers can evolve their communication to be noticeably more engaging—and even measure the varying customer perspectives to improve the content. Something like the X Optimizer GPT, meanwhile, can not only tweak your social media posts but also identify the optimal times to post them on your channel.

Another content use case is supportive in nature. This includes generating research polls, allowing multilingualism for a wider geographic or cultural expanse, and rendering relevant responses to customer queries—another form of process automation. A tool like Video GPT can generate a user guide video from your available training materials, in your voice—all in a matter of minutes!

A great example of visual amplification is the gorgeous AI art created by Refik Anadol and displayed at the Museum of Modern Art (MoMA) in New York.[6] One can easily see such an application being used in promotions or product displays, accomplished by tools like Im2Go and NightCafe with simple text prompts or even existing images.

Marketing optimization: In light of the ability to generate such a wide variety of content, its optimization is a crucial area where generative AI can help. Sticking with Google's example, Performance Max can help create and scale new assets quickly. But the market is evolving fast, and techniques like LCM-LoRA (Latent Consistency Model—Low Rank Adaptation) can speed up content generation so much that it effectively happens in real time. This allows tools like Krea.ai or Fal.ai to generate content that responds to our actions by inducing the corresponding changes in an image simultaneously.

LCM-LoRA has immediate applicability in video games, other virtual, augmented, and mixed-reality use cases, and even video production. Consider a streetside billboard where a character in an advertisement moves with its subject through its length, striking a conversation for better engagement and persuasiveness.

Optimization similarly implies quicker A/B testing and generation of ad variants while an online campaign is running. That's what the tool Predict by Neurons can accomplish for you, allowing better brand building and markedly improved awareness and engagement from your marketing spend.

Dessert

Our journey through content enablement with AI has helped us chart a pathway to improved content maturity. Whether it's text, images, videos, sounds, hybrid files, codes, or entire entities, we have seen how different content types can merge or even help generate each other with generative AI. These impressions can not only help produce effective material at scale—from planning to execution—but also allow improved audience engagement. Such optimization brings us to the doorstep of automation and insights enablement. Let us now proceed to look at how productivity and effectiveness of every resource hour and dollar spent by marketing can be exponentially improved with generative AI-based automation, thereby gifting a competitive advantage that necessitates the technology's adoption by every other player in the market.

CHAPTER 9

Generative AI Automation

Entrée

What's better than to create and leverage attractive content quickly and at scale? It is to automate doing so. AI-enabled automation encapsulates what makes AI so powerful: a system that can perform tasks autonomously at an unmatched scale and speed. This attribute of generative AI is not limited to generating content alone; in fact, it has a greater impact on processes. This chapter introduces vital cogs in the application of generative AI, for some measure of process enablement is always involved in these initiatives. As a first step, we will look at how to identify opportunities for automation in an organization from the many possibilities that are typically available. The chapter then discusses techniques and examples to guide us on how to execute the automation agenda.

Due to a deluge of calls, e-mails, and repetitive tasks like data entry and document filing, most professionals typically spend less than half their time on productive work. The collateral impact of nonstimulating work only adds to how effective we are in the little time we spend on the more productive tasks. So, for knowledge workers, job displacement concerns aside, AI can free up time to improve engagement and productivity levels.

Automation improves productivity in a variety of other ways. Saving lives, for one. Think about the hazardous task in a steel manufacturing plant that a robot or drone can assist with, while the worker assigned to it can now shift to operating the machine itself. With use cases like these existing aplenty in any organization, our first step is to determine where the opportunities for automation potentially exist today.

Automation Opportunities

There are several factors that can point us to not only the need but also the feasibility of successful automation. It can be deployed across the marketing organization, specific project areas, or even a cluster of tasks within one area. Accordingly, its impact can also stretch across these levels. Any complexity is mostly introduced by the multilevel coordination that is often needed as a result. This is why having an Automation functional group allows better alignment of initiatives across the project areas.

The idea is not meant to discourage siloed automation but to enable it to take place in an informed manner. This is important to ensure that one automation step does not interfere with (or duplicate) other processes and systems. For instance, tasks related to social media posting within the Awareness project area may have unique automation requirements—and opportunities—that are not applicable to social media-related tasks within the Customer Support project area. Conversely, this automation—say, to monitor how people are reacting to a post—may also be crucial to some of the customer support tasks. In the latter case, an automation may find better utility if applied to tasks within both areas, thereby improving its ROI.

So, how can we assess what can be automated and whether an automation will help and not hinder us? Here are some of the factors to consider.

Cost: The first—and most important factor—can easily be an umbrella term covering several others that follow. In this case, it refers to existing costs that an organization could save on. These include time-taking, repetitive tasks that absorb the workforce. It can also include software subscriptions that may no longer be the most efficient. Automation can often help reduce existing costs in an organization by speeding up the time a bottleneck process takes or increasing the volumes of orders processed to bring in more revenue.

Resources: While automation can be seen as a way to curb resource costs, most organizations automate tasks to deal with an existing resource crunch and maximize what the current team can deliver. The organization may have the necessary capital to hire more people but given the time it would take to train more people, the inefficiencies that even new resources would have to face, and the risks of eventual churn, an investment in a specific automation may be deemed more prudent.

Skillset: Automation can close a gap in the skillset and improve resource productivity. However, it can also fail to deliver if the team is not skilled enough to manage such automation. The time, cost, and feasibility of upskilling resources must all be taken into consideration. A review of the skillset can reveal which processes can be feasibly automated.

Competitive weakness and strength: An organization can enjoy a significant competitive advantage, particularly if there's competitor weakness or a market gap that automation helps take advantage of. It can also be essential—regardless of the costs and other barriers involved—to keep pace with the competition if the other players are leveraging automation to steer ahead. The simplest example is your competitor automating discounts to offer an online shopper to avoid abandoned carts on its website. In other words, an assessment of opportunities and threats can offer a strong reason to pursue automation. The result could range from carving a new niche to ensuring survival for the company in a competitive landscape.

Sustainability: Often overlooked, the sustainability of an automation should never be discounted. Let's say your team subscribes to a new solution automating customer insight generation from sales conversations, but your sales team neither has the time nor the intention to feed the details of their prospect conversations into the system. Even if they are trained to, and begin to do so, the enthusiasm eventually dies out, the solution gets deprioritized or is minimally used because it takes up too much time. In either case, proper utilization tends to be lacking. So, the sustainability of a potential automation is important to qualify whether and when it should be taken up.

Stack and cost overload: A direct result of the scenario above is often the pile-up of redundant solutions and mounting subscription costs. Even for automations that are leveraged well, incoherence in their planning and deployment can introduce inefficiencies instead of taking them out. Let's say a team automates steps A and B, unaware of a second team that had automated steps B and C. The organization will then be faced with not only a redundancy in automating step B but also the risk of two solutions not working together. In other words, the additional investment may hamper step B. On the other hand, successful automations can also negate the issue of stack and cost overload, particularly if the systems can be integrated to create a seamless informational flow.

Barriers from or to existing systems/processes: Let's say that the second team in the example above now comes across a new solution that can cost-effectively automate step A. It now has to make one of the three choices: It could automate step A with a new solution that would add redundancies and costs; abandon its own automation and process to allow synchronization with the other team; or accept the overhead of continuing to execute step A manually. If an automation either interferes with existing systems and processes or limits an organization's flexibility to introduce new ones in the future, it may be better to think twice.

Workforce support: Whether it's the leadership or the rest of the organization, an automation needs buy-in from all. Even for a state-of-the-art automation solution that can improve efficiencies, if the leadership support is missing, it is unlikely to gain traction. This is not only in the case of insufficient budget allocation but also when the executives do not understand the technology well enough to lend their weight to it. The appetite to establish an automation's requirement of appropriate processes and policies to prosper and the leadership's appetite to establish these are important determinants of adoption and returns on the investment.

Low adoption can also be due to a lack of employee support, particularly if an employee is unclear on how an automation will help her, feels at risk of being replaced, or simply does not have the time to prioritize supporting the system. The problem can also simply be disillusionment if, say, an organization has tried several solutions or changes before without much success. People rarely like changes, especially when they are frequent or unclear on their value.

Collateral impact: The collateral impact of automation can often be soft or indirect. While job loss is one to estimate in advance, it is equally important to estimate the impact on an organization's brand, customer satisfaction, and other such factors. For example, job losses can hamper an employer's reputation, whereas inappropriate customer support responses from a chatbot can lead to disgruntled customers. Similarly, automated e-mails can get marked as spam and lower the company's domain reputation and future e-mail deliverability, whereas automated social media posting on a day of some social tragedy can come across as insensitive and hurt the brand.

This last one brings us to a different aspect of automation decision making. While the factors mentioned so far help assess the impact of automation, the next four factors help determine whether the chosen tasks can be automated reliably.

Repeatability or rule-logic: Automation works best for tasks that are repetitive and follow certain logical rules that can be programmed. This is why automation was first introduced in the production lines of manufacturing companies, long before artificial intelligence took hold of our industries. Each one of us has portions of our job that do not require a lot of brainwork. Data entry in a CRM tool is a prime example, which is why many solutions today have automated populating first-party or third-party information on customer contacts in the CRM.

Predictability: Rule-based automation can hit a snag in unpredictable situations. If a task deals with such situations often, it may not be automation-friendly. Conversely, tasks that are mostly always predictable or at least have a predictable rule of execution to deal with unpredictable situations serve as a good starting point for automation. Take customer chatbots as a familiar example. Customer questions are not always predictable but can reliably be bucketed into a few support areas. This is why call centers constitute high levels of automation that enable them to handle larger volumes. Any occasional anomaly in the question asked can then automatically redirect the customer to a human agent.

Criticality: Even among tasks that rarely face unpredictable situations, automation opportunities may be limited if the task is critical to the business and errors may prove too costly. Tasks that involve such decision making or situations critical to the business are best kept under the visibility and control of people accountable for them. Automation may still be applied but would have to be designed to always be humanly monitored or to alert the users in case of the slightest anomaly.

Intuitiveness and sentiment: Finally, tasks that are more *human* in nature in requiring the use of sentiment and intuition are best executed by people. It has been the foundational differentiator between humans and machines to date. It is not simply a matter of capability as AI is becoming better every day to deal with emotional or subjective tasks—from board seats to investment analysis for venture capital firms to offering companionship for lonely humans. Nonetheless, there are several instances where an organization would still be better placed to have a human handle some of these because of the optics and subjective risks at play.

Say a customer's credit card was declined while trying to get medicines in a foreign country. While the system may reject the transaction for it looking fishy on account of the location, the customer may have an urgent need to access funds that automation may not allow. In a different case, a customer support agent in a call center may show no urgency for an automation to take note of but be at risk of a serious mental health issue due to the customer complaints she is constantly exposed to. Back in the boardroom of an enterprise firm, a system may see good value in a company being targeted for acquisition but completely miss out on a potential cultural misfit.

Many of the tasks that were formerly considered far too important to automate have now been handed over to systems nonetheless. That is what progression toward an artificial general intelligence (AGI) looks like. What stands in the way of automating such tasks then is our comfort level. That is likely to develop too, as people become more familiar and accustomed to the use of AI in various tasks at home and work. After all, while we are hesitant or apprehensive to automate a task, watching our neighbor at home or competitor at work do so can prove to be a strong influencer.

The good thing about generative AI is that we can also directly ask a tool like ChatGPT to recommend tasks that can be automated, whether a particular unique one can be automated, and what successful industry examples of a particular automation look like. The right prompts—laden with clarity on our business context, the processes involved, the current challenges, and our objective—is likely to produce a list of automations to address the challenge or meet our objectives. We can then analyze those options against the factors discussed earlier to decide which one is worth pursuing.

Automation Techniques

At the end of the day, any automation should improve productivity and efficiency, helping an organization control its costs or scale revenues sustainably. Generative AI simply expands the ways in which that can be accomplished successfully—from the complex (e.g., code development) to the frequent (e.g., file conversions) to the critical (e.g., customer interactions). With its current advances, they can even create new generative AI tools.

Organizations typically have one of three options to automate a process: build a tool, connect to an existing one, or use an existing one directly. This in turn can lead to a generative AI application, Application Programming Interface (APIs) connected to existing models, or a proprietary large language model built in-house or subscribed to. These are the three common automation techniques.

1. **Using generative AI applications:** We discussed Google's Performance Max in the last chapter to help edit, test, and scale advertising content on the go. Likewise, there's Article Forge to write articles, BeFunky to create images, Audialab to create drumbeats, and so many more that can not only automate and speed up creation but also offer a better way of doing so. Consider an application like Convert Anything, which can allow a team to convert one file to another.

This automation can help organizations avoid the risk of uploading (and sharing) proprietary files with third-party websites.

Microsoft Copilot can take our work with these files a step further, automating a vast variety of tasks on MS Office applications. Thanks to its Bing and Dall-E integrations, we can now create stellar depictions of data on a presentation or perform those expert calculations and data analyses that have long been the domain of Excel magicians. It can summarize meetings on Teams or e-mail trails on Outlook. It can even draft entire documents on Word and generate Dall-E images to upload into other Office applications.

What Copilot is effectively creating, slowly but surely, is *generative AI as an experience*. It is the automation of our routine work on computers. Apple has followed suit in its ecosystem, turning laptops into a system running on integrated generative AI applications. Samsung's Gauss, Google's Gemini, and Amazon's Q are all having their say in this ever-growing race already.

2. **Connecting to existing models or tools:** Why build an LLM when you can simply use a pre-existing one? The introduction of the RAG concept mentioned earlier can allow a company to use tools like ChatGPT but limit its responses to proprietary information that the company uploads into the system. They help bring the best of two worlds—low-cost existing LLM plugged into first-party UI and data.

The concept is put to great use by companies like GPT Crawler, Lyris, and Chatbase, all of which allow companies to build their own GPT chatbots. While Lyris is specific to answering AI sales and support questions—from pricing to training, Chatbase has a wider domain range. We can feed in a website URL or upload our own PDF, for instance, to get a chatbot capable of answering questions based on that information.

Today, we have a plethora of solutions connected to ChatGPT in the backend. Such API connections can supercharge AI automation. That is why we now have entire generative AI marketplaces like GenAI.works that are filled with apps for just about any use case, most leveraging a common LLM.

For tools that cannot be directly connected, Zapier (or other online automation tools like it) can come to the rescue. Such integrations help ensure that a marketing team can connect a tool like ChatGPT to an existing application that now reads a customer e-mail, generates a response, and e-mails it back automatically.

Amazon's Q is another example. While Copilot can be specific to the Web or Microsoft applications, Q can bring GPT functionality of prompts and answers to other software applications like Slack, Salesforce, Dropbox, and even Microsoft 365 that its AWS customers may be using.

What automation is heading toward is giving us personalized AI agents that can execute our tasks on software applications and beyond. For example, Ebi.ai can be used to create such customer assistants in minutes, as can Chatwith. But Auto-GPT, built on OpenAI's GPT models, offers an AI agent that can generate its own prompts to accomplish tasks. That includes using search engines to not only find but also verify data. Its aim is to perform tasks with minimal input from the user. And yes, that means it can write its own codes.

3. **Building a proprietary generative AI app or large language model:** The customization offered by companies like OpenAI to chatbots built using their LLM can be quite comprehensive. Yet, not all generative AI tools performing the same function do so equally well. If one looks at some of the popular chatbots, some are more creative than others but may not be as accurate or relevant in their output. This is perhaps why Microsoft's Bing introduced a scale allowing generative content to range from more creative to more precise. The same is true for avoiding AI hallucinations where certain tools are known to perform better than others.

Tools are continuously evolving, which is why their competitiveness across these different parameters can change over time. The alternative, for teams that have the resources to afford it, is to generate their own LLM or applications. Such proprietary products can allow a team to better incorporate its own identity. That can work wonderfully in keeping the user experience consistent with the brand identity. X's Grok, for example, often has a funny angle to its responses.

Such models can be built using existing libraries. There are several on Python, for instance—TensorFlow for text, image, or music generation; Acme, which utilizes reinforcement learning to perform generative AI tasks; LlamaIndex, which can help manage large amounts of data with searchable generative AI models; and Weights & Biases, which can manage different generative AI experiments.

Libraries can vary depending on their performance and clarity, as well as the amount of data or coding skills they require. So, the sophistication of LLM build may be too much for some organizations. The approach then is to utilize open-source LLMs like Microsoft's Phi-2, Meta's Llama, Mistral, or Hugging Face to build applications more easily. The programming skillset required here is different from the one needed to generate codes for creative content. This is why data and MLOps engineers are likely to be found in the Automation functional group, even though the data scientists may come from the Insights group.

The automation trend with the development that started with libraries of prewritten codes has progressed to one of not only prewritten models (LLMs, in this case) but also no-code apps. Applications, after all, go beyond just the codes. They involve the user interface, user experience, access, and iteration. AI can automate the coding part. OpenAI's GPT-4 Vision is a fantastic example here. It powers apps like SwiftUI which can create an app (i.e., generate HTML) from a simple drawing and the right prompts. The drawing could be a user interface, known applications like a calculator, or even entire functionalities depicted in a workflow.

Fine-tuning of proprietary LLMs for different use cases can also imply high computational costs. As we will see later in the book, solutions like S-LoRA are changing that fast by bringing the costs down significantly. Nonetheless, the onus of preventing hallucinations and jailbreak prompts would still rest with the organization.

Automation Examples

Let us reflect on an automated marketing journey for an art-and-craft company's online store. It begins with market research. An Auto-GPT-enabled tool can gather and analyze third-party data on a market opportunity or trends in play to help the company assess the evolving market demand. Such prebuilt generative AI can then look at the company's first-party product information and recommend a niche offering from its catalog of products and capabilities.

Next, we bring the content creators to communicate the product value to its buyers. They begin with Chromax to present ideas as visual stories of the chosen offer. The team can then utilize tools like Vision to generate a landing page for this offer on their website. It's now time for promotional campaigns. Eye for AI can offer the right prompts to generate desired images from the web page text already in place, as can G-Prompter. Hour One can then create presenter-led videos from that existing content. ChatGPT produces blogs, which Adori Labs can pick up to create additional videos. Capsule edits them.

Now we bring in Google Gemini to watch and summarize these videos (if on YouTube) and recommend ways to improve their visibility. TubeBuddy could do something similar. Once finalized, HeyGen's tool will allow the video coverage to become globally relevant as it not only converts videos into other languages but even changes our lip movements in the video to be in sync with the foreign words. FeedHive can take it from here by helping create and manage AI content for social media at scale—from podcasts to posts. Performance Max meanwhile will help optimize the ad copies that leverage this content.

Meanwhile, our art-and-craft company connects its e-mail outreach solution to ChatGPT via Zapier (if a direct integration does not already exist). This allows them not only to craft effective e-mails but also to receive and read customer replies to generate and send a personalized response.

We finally arrive at the moment of purchase for a customer. Consider a prompt that generates a code to automate buying a stock every time its price falls 20 percent and selling it when the price increases by 50 percent from the purchase price. The same logic could be applied to induce a custom product discount for customers, offering a 20 percent reduction on the new product upon certain behavioral or temporal triggers.

Once the purchase is done, these customers need support. This is where the team can explore building a language model based on historical customer support chat data to automate future query handling. And since the sequence of marketing initiatives based on their interdependencies is key to their success, ChatGPT could create an Eisenhower matrix (where the urgency of tasks is mapped against their importance) to better prioritize them for us.

This is just one extended example of executing automation across multiple use cases to achieve an eventual goal—generating incremental revenue. Instead of conducting market research to identify new opportunities, the art-and-craft company could create a model that analyzes a customer's online shopping cart to determine what art or craft she may like to create. It could then auto-recommend the missing items in that predicted creation as a way to upsell to her. Unlike the typical recommendation engines, which recommend items closely associated with those already in the cart, such a model would expand the possibilities to products not directly associated, thereby appealing to the shopper's creativity.

Companies, of course, are using automations in varied ways. They can be just as helpful in enhancing customer experience and by extension, customer loyalty. Take Walmart's Text to Shop[1] which allows customers to text their orders, allowing them to, say, add items to their order while they are en route for pickup. British AI firm Luminance, meanwhile, has leveraged its own LLM to build Autopilot—a tool that can analyze and even negotiate a contract on its own, eliminating a lot of paperwork for lawyers.[2]

The beauty of generative AI automation is that even one person can often get it done. For example, this author set up a three-layer automation to drive sales engagement at his company—from lead sourcing to its segmentation, multichannel outreach, follow-ups, and even replies. Ben Parr, cofounder and president of a zero-party data marketing platform called Octane AI, created VCGPT,[3] a GPT he trained to be a venture capitalist that start-up founders could use to improve their investor pitch decks.[4] Amy Merrywest, founder of Pitch & Shout PR, has crafted her own prompting approach which entrepreneurs can use on ChatGPT to produce customized press releases that could maximize coverage.[5]

Automation can get a lot done, and at scale, but it does need monitoring and some consideration. Care is needed to not overdo it. Scalability should still be at a level manageable by people. To understand this better, let's take the sales engagement automation example above. One of the steps was to *like* our prospects' LinkedIn posts before sending a message or connection request. Now, if one went overboard with the sudden liking of multiple posts on a LinkedIn account, its owner would immediately know that it's a bot visiting her profile. Consequently, our authenticity would be lost even before we have had a chance to connect with her.

Similar is the case with overpersonalization which could risk sounding inaccurate when executed at scale. For example, if an automation is designed to cite an individual's current role based on an existing dataset, we must take care to ensure the database is regularly updated to capture role transitions. Otherwise, the recipient may receive an e-mail citing his former role at another company. A better way to personalize may be to capture the conversational personality (which tends to be more permanent than temporary career data) of the individual and craft messages accordingly—another subjective parameter that has been made more accessible by generative AI.

Dessert

Automation can lower cost and improve returns—two essentials to sustain competitivity. That's the battery powering its rise to the forefront of organizational AI enablements. With little to no distinguishing boundaries between distinct automation opportunities, it is important to qualify them carefully based on their costs and risks and resulting returns. Automation-friendly tasks tend to score higher on being rule-based and predictable and lower on their use of sentiment and criticality to the business. Once pursued, automation can be achieved directly with pre-existing applications, built on those, or built from scratch.

Whether it is set up to generate content or improve productivity, a natural output of automated systems is the insights they can gift companies. That, in fact, is often the underlying objective to automate something because as we saw in Part 2 of this book, hidden insights require deeper pattern recognition to surface, which in turn requires an automated analysis of large volumes of data. It is time now to turn our attention to the third functional group—Insights.

CHAPTER 10

Generative AI Insights

Entrée

When it's not generating creative content, generative AI is busy generating insights. One may even say that it's always doing the latter. In many of the automation examples we discussed in the previous chapter, insights were a necessary ingredient (in optimizing social media posts, for example) or the desired output (in the initial research). If AI's strength is in pattern recognition, and generative AI brings the deep learning-level capability of recognizing complex and indiscernible patterns, then insights have to be its strongest output. Everything else it does is just an application of that strength. In this chapter, we will explore the value levers of these insights and look at measurements and contextuality—two ways in which the value is realized.

Insights Value

The value insights bring through informational empowerment can be carved in several ways. Here are five major ones:

Strategy and Planning: At the very top of a go-to-market journey is the overarching goal setting, which requires insights into the market dynamics, consumer trends, organizational gaps, and revenue and cost realities. The marketing goal is often a product of aligning those insights with the corporate strategy. It is what leads to the formulation of a business strategy if marketing has that say in an organization. Even if it doesn't, the insights can help validate and improve the strength of the business strategy, which can lead to a robust marketing strategy.

An overall strategy helps the project areas within marketing to prepare their own plans to execute their respective roles in the overall strategy. It can lead to silos which introduce cracks in the strategy execution. However, if these project areas have individuals from the Insights functional group carrying a close understanding of the overall marketing strategy and, more importantly, the goal it is trying to meet (since they were the ones who helped formulate it), pan-domain alignment becomes much simpler.

Business Casing: Any strategic goal carved from the insights requires a convincing business case to ensure executive buy-in and budget allocation, particularly in larger companies. A business case typically comprises the scope of an initiative, the investment involved, and the benefits to be expected. The benefits are determined by the delta (difference) between the desired state that will be achieved with this investment and the current state that will continue to exist without it. This is the other area where generative AI insights can help.

The current state of a company is best reflected in its proprietary data of financial results, customer feedback, resource realities, product capability information, and other such in-house documents. The desired state, meanwhile, can often be derived from credible third-party sources. This can include market research from leading organizations or proven evidentiary information of organizations in the industry who attempted the planned initiative and succeeded.

As may be apparent, a lot of the information going into the current and desired state assessments is subjective or relies on the collation of data from diverse sources. Cue: Generative AI. Many of the tools we have discussed in the previous two chapters can help make sense of the information and even craft the differential benefit between the two states, thereby helping build the business case for a marketing initiative or strategic shift—a necessary step if marketers want to turn insights into a market winning strategy.

Execution Efficiency: Remember the aforementioned movie line from *Oppenheimer* on all minds having to see the whole task to contribute efficiently? Execution efficiency is a central reason why

AI-driven organizations need to rethink their operational structures today.

Let us go back to how an Insights functional group enables better cross-project alignment by percolating resources across these areas. A project may be an ongoing one—say, to manage online awareness and engagements—or one formed temporarily—say, to deal with a credibility crisis or to organize a conference. Whatever their longevity, project teams need clarity of purpose as they shift and swell in order to formulate their own subplan. The Insights resources can not only bring that clarity to a project team but also relay this team's consequent plan, progress, and results (insights) back to their functional group to align their peers who are part of the other project teams.

Execution efficiency refers to the versatility it can offer to each project team to customize their initiatives to changing situations, personalize them for the subsegments of their audience, and scale over time. Insights can help predict situational changes or demand fluctuations. They can also help better profile customers down to an individual buyer and alert the team on their changing shopping behaviors as their life circumstances change.

Status Tracking: Keeping track of just how efficient an execution has been and what may be needed is where measurement becomes mandatory. Whether to make the initial business case, recommend a subsequent shift in direction, or validate the performance of initiatives against the organizational expectations, every team must be able to churn out measures that the Insights resources can assimilate at their functional level to produce the overall measures against the organizational goals. Metrics become synonymous with insights here, as we will see shortly.

There are several attempts ongoing at automating the current state analysis of an organization's operations. Such bots could assess systems, interview stakeholders, and report on the state of data, security risks, or even gaps in the technology stack. Sounds too fanciful? It's a matter of time before such an automated insights generation becomes a reality.

Approach Agility: Insights coming out of the status tracking mentioned earlier will likely always require agility to adapt proactively. Insights from preinstalled systems or from those executing initiatives can help reformulate strategies and course-correct the marketing direction significantly quicker than otherwise possible. Imagine the social media team discovering that the niche identified by the Insights group originally is incorrect—perhaps a case of misinterpreted data. Any assumptions made in the planning phase get tested during execution and reacting quickly to mistakes can be the difference between millions of dollars wasted or recovered.

The ability to pivot dynamically is a dream few organizations can realize today, even in startups and small organizations. That is because having the right intent here is not enough. One needs solid data backing on the current state gaps or emerging risks or opportunities to commit to a change and avoid, as they say, throwing the baby out with the bath water.

In a similar vein to the automation journey, insights generation can play a key role along the marketing journey. Where automation's primary benefit was productivity, insights bring efficiency, though neither benefit is mutually exclusive. Most marketing journey insights have two requirements to effectively track and improve the performance of marketing initiatives: the right metrics set by marketing, as discussed earlier, and an ability for LLMs to analyze proprietary data. Let us now look at each element involved in comprehensive insight generation.

Measurement Consideration

It is incredible how deeply and comprehensively a marketing team can review measures and drivers of success (or failure) as a result of the new organizational structure. Insights are otherwise seldom deep enough to reveal the root causes of what's working or not. They can also rarely be matched across teams to determine who missed the ball.

This takes us back to one of the very first examples we discussed in this book. Let's reimagine Silver Water, the water softener company's launch of a new offer that its different marketing teams worked to promote, sell, and support through advertisements, inbound call agents, sales representatives, and technicians. Instead of hypothesizing and searching for the root cause of low sales, what if the corporate office had resources accountable for bringing insights from each of these areas involved? Assimilating them would have not only shown the drop in sales but also tied it to the call agent insights that revealed the bottleneck. How many dollars might have been saved and earned in this scenario?

Insights generated from an AI tool can be used to acquire elusive information more efficiently or to justify the investment in the tool itself. Either way, their relevance is closely linked to the metrics or the key performance indicators (KPIs) chosen by the team. The KPIs used with generative AI often follow the standard marketing measures, at least at the macro strategic level set by the Insights functional group. The operational level that dictates what each project area should focus on, and the consequent initiatives taken up by these teams are where metrics become more generative AI-focused.

Much like the organizational structure within marketing, the metrics also need some rethinking. Two omnichannel measuring techniques that have been making a comeback among organizations to better optimize ad spend across channels are the Multitouch Attribution (MTA) Model and Marketing Mix Modeling (MMM). This is partly due to the difficulty of tracking personally identifiable information like cookies in the light of stricter privacy regulations. *That's odd*, one may argue; in the age of generative AI, shouldn't insights become more custom and personalized?

We certainly are getting there though in different ways. The regulations can be considered a shot in the arm for the use of generative AI to generate insights—one that has compelled teams to look beyond the old ways of tracking behaviors. Sticking with ad spends, the objective for online advertisers is to spend in a way that maximizes views, clicks, or purchases on their website. So, while they lose out on pixel data and cookies, they can now leverage generative AI tools for something even better—real-time understanding of behaviors and predictability of the ad performance.

That is what Neurons' tool Predict has achieved. Replacing Web browsing behaviors with elusive neuroscience data, it can perform A/B tests on ad varieties, fine-tuning, and launch of the best predicted performing ad.

If it can drive 55 percent higher conversions, 42 percent higher engagement, 29.5 percent higher click-through rates, and 20 percent higher awareness—as the customer success stories on its website state as of the time of this writing[1]—would the advertiser still miss the older ways of tracking?

Not all generative AI-enabled metrics have to use sophisticated approaches like neuroscience. In a sponsored release on *The Wall Street Journal's* CMO Today, Deloitte shared the onset of Granular MMM[2] as the metric of choice in the age of AI. According to the article, Granular MMM would look at "aggregated media spend and impressions data; non-marketing information such as seasonality, competition, and economic conditions; and customer transactional and experience data," thereby not only achieving relevant and real-time insights but also avoiding personally identifiable information.

Qloo is another great example of a tool that provides contextualized personalization based on the behavioral correlations of not just people but places and things—hundreds of millions of them. So a company doesn't have to individually track what movies and restaurants you like but what restaurant preferences closely follow certain movie genres. The next time any unidentified person is watching a certain movie, the corresponding restaurant ad can be shown to them.

The bottom line is this: Privacy regulations and the simultaneous arrival of generative AI have laid the groundwork to move marketers to more advanced ways of improving performance. If cookies helped elucidate what a customer did on her laptop browser, generative AI can help elucidate what she may want to do next without necessarily identifying her. If cookies helped offer the ingredients for an organization to determine the best recipe for an ad in a given population, generative AI can both automate and create that recipe for segments within that population.

Netomi's CEO Puneet Mehta underscored generative AI's gift of delivering a personally relevant experience without using personally identifiable information when he explained how the technology brings information that marketers have historically not had access to. Such deep personalization helps achieve a far more intimate customer experience. And intimacy is a fantastic way to develop loyalty.

Mr. Mehta was speaking at the Mars Agency's ShopTalk 2023,[3] which also featured several other marketing experts and their take on generative AI. Colgate-Palmolive's Diana Haussling, for one, stressed how the company is able to better understand trends and react. What that implies is achieving relevance and the agility needed to sustain it over time—another vital contribution of insights from generative AI.

These companies have excavated value from insights in areas they had earmarked as their main goal. That is why the choice of metrics can make such a difference. But it is not the only determinant of successful insights generation. The use case specificity and technology matter too, which is where the right prompts as well as the right tools become important, as we will see next.

Contextuality Consideration

Much like automation, generative AI's insights can cover a broad spectrum of use cases. While most are generic—rendered specific only by the rigor of the prompts—and simply utilize external third-party information available on the open Web, the ones more relevant to the chosen metrics are likely to come from an organization's own data.

Generic insights first. With ChatGPT alone, we can use the five-why technique to get to the root cause of a problem, request analogies or visual representations to better understand something, or get counterarguments to defeat an assessment. It could analyze the competitive market for our product, identify a niche and its corresponding value proposition, help us validate our strategy against it, and create a business model that is likely to work better. We can even directly ask the tool to share the best practices and factors that led to companies that succeeded in our industry.

ChatGPT even has dedicated tools to help with insights generation from specific sources. ResearchGPT, for example, can scan and review academic papers and, of course, extract answers or citations from them. Its Market Analyst Pro, on the other hand, can scan market trends to help with trading strategies for stock market investors.

While the examples above leverage information from external sources, the marketing insights linked to the team's chosen metrics would require the analysis of proprietary organizational data or very specific third-party information. That is where RAG helps.

Retrieval-augmented generation (RAG) is the ability of LLM to accept and analyze proprietary data of a user to generate custom and relevant responses. It allows organizations to build custom chatbots from existing applications like Lyris, Chatbase, or ChatGPT as we discussed earlier. The same principle applies to nonchatbot applications designed to provide information on a different but specific set of data.

Suppose the customer support team wants to improve efficiencies by resolving some of the most common recurring customer concerns. A RAG application can scan the dataset of all customer interactions to date on the company website, e-mails, chatbot, or transcribed phone calls to recognize and produce the most common pain points, their context, and conditions in which they arise, in a jiffy. What's more, thanks to generative AI's expertise at interpreting subjective data, it can also reveal which of those concerns seem controllable by the customer support team, effectively allowing them to focus on the critical few issues that the team can resolve once and for all.

Textual analysis with RAG can be taken a step further. Besides looking at market trends and academic papers, it could analyze newspaper articles on a topic from across the globe in order to find the variances in perspectives captured, contradictory information published, or even factual anomalies. For a marketing team of a global organization, that would enable it to quickly grasp the public standing internationally, and geographies that may need additional support to either rectify its brand image or capitalize on an opportunity.

Document and image analysis follows the same concept. A generative AI tool can be given a chatbot interface to allow users to simply ask for information based on the data uploaded by them. This is what OpenAI enabled with its PDF chat feature, where you could upload a document to then ask for insights exclusively from the content therein. The direct questioning ability extends to images as well. Upload an image and circle the part we'd like ChatGPT to focus on, and it can answer questions around it.

The questioning enablement is not limited to the marketing team alone. A tool like Chatsimple could ingest our website data from a URL to engage the website visitors, better understand what they want, and promote our services accordingly. With its ability to personalize responses to each individual, it somewhat fills the shoes of both a salesperson and a call center agent.

Such a RAG ability activates a personal assistant for any user— employee or customer. For it to work well today and to avoid overwhelming the LLM, it is advised that data be fed in smaller chunks instead of in a single large file (e.g., uploading individual chapters instead of the entire book). Used optimally, it can serve as a learning tool or extract important or required information in a specific context.

The direct impact is the speed with which one can move on to the next task, effectively lowering the time and cost involved. The same is true for more sophisticated data analysis or presenting information, say, in a graphical manner—be it spider plots, pie charts, bar charts, line graphs, flowcharts, or even A/B test results. WizeCharts, Noteable, Graph Constructor, AnyBarChart, Mermaid Chart, A/B Chart, and Eraser are all plugins that can come in handy in this use case.

Graphs can be helpful in managing keywords for search engine optimization too. Let's bring back the case of our art-and-craft company rolling out a new holiday offer. It now has a web page built exclusively for this offer and would like to make it SEO-friendly. We have already seen how the technology can reveal market trends or trending topics on social media to use in the website content for SEO. We have also had AI solutions like CallRail's Conversation Intelligence that could further help zero down on keywords that come up most frequently in conversations that the team has with its customers.

SEO is a vast topic to cover but ChatGPT has enabled individuals to create custom applications with this technology. Consider the custom GSC Keyword Ranking Changes Scatter Plot tool built on ChatGPT that can plot changes in the rankings of keywords to help focus on the right ones. On-page SEO analyzer can then test this page against the short-listed keywords that the team provides, ensuring it has used the relevant terms effectively, while Search Quality GPT can assess content against the experience, expertise, authoritativeness, and trustworthiness factors which Google tracks to rank pages. Competitive Analysis AI can then compare that against what the competitors are doing. Armed with these insights, the company can then improve the content using any of the many tools we discussed earlier.

Of course, Google is not sitting idle through all this, having updated its search engine with its generative AI capability that focuses on directly answering a user's queries. Nonetheless, the beauty of these tools is that they exemplify how able marketing organizations can build one for their unique use case if one doesn't exist already. They don't necessarily require coding expertise. On the contrary, they can often take matters out of IT and empower every user—be it an individual or a team—to address their needs. The industry is actively working toward making this a reality. What we have to watch out for then are the risks that such ubiquitous enablement can bring with it—something we have discussed at length already.

Dessert

Insights can be derived from most things that generative AI does. They could be used at every step of a marketing process—from conception and planning to execution and feedback. While generative AI is making predictive actions and their measurement possible, techniques like RAG allow relevance in the insights a team gets from these systems. Earlier in the book, I had mentioned that generative AI has made marketing even more analytical and data-driven at the cost of a purely creative focus. Having turned so many stones otherwise scattered around generative AI enablement, it is now that the claim can be improvised.

The truth is that generative AI's data focus is making the field more creative in a different way. Creativity now rests in our prompts, in how we generate entire applications for unique use cases, in how we integrate them to automate work, and yes, in how we evolve existing or AI-generated content. In that sense, the sky's the limit on how a team can analyze data or leverage it to achieve the marketing objectives set by the functional groups or the project areas. How high does that sky reach? In the next part, we will attempt at some of the oncoming changes generative AI is likely to witness.

PART 4

Bringing It All Together

You cannot escape the responsibility of tomorrow by evading it today.
—Abraham Lincoln

Congratulations on having traversed the generative AI journey we have been on so far. There's a lot we have unpacked across two distinct but rapidly fusing fields of marketing and AI. Mapping all the technological and managerial shifts in pursuing revenue growth with generative AI effectively cloaks the undercurrents of an organizational redefinition. Those at the heart of it and in the know will invariably be the ones who lead this generational endeavor. For signaling your willingness to take that responsibility as you picked this book in your hands, take a bow.

This final part of the book houses two chapters that are polar opposites. The first aims to further expand the boundaries of what we have learnt so far with a look into the future. We will discuss the implications of generative AI innovation and paint a reality that will likely be a small subset of what manifests. The second chapter will embrace these far reaches as well as the reality already in play to summarize everything. In doing so, it will lend a final context on what our generative AI world is and how we can begin to lead it in an optimal manner.

Ready for a final flight?

CHAPTER 11

What Comes Next

Entrée

Predicting the future is a fanciful job. Even if it's an informed estimation, it is rendered meaningful only by the strength of its underlying patterns. A generative AI future can go in many directions, impacted by macroeconomic factors we may not yet foresee. What we do know is the large-scale operational automation it is likely to bring to companies, thanks to improvements in its underlying models. Those same improvements will also give birth to novel applications which were elusive earlier. All of that will inevitably result in a socioeconomic shift, similar to what the first Industrial Revolution, the arrival of cars, or the rise of social media did. A host of macroeconomic or geopolitical events can prolong its trajectory but we are likely to keep heading toward an artificial general intelligence reality. In this chapter, we will expand on the ongoing changes to paint a picture of tomorrow in an as unassuming way as is feasible.

The World Science Festival in 2023 saw the renowned author and physicist Brian Greene moderating a panel on AI as part of The Big Ideas Series, supported in part by the John Templeton Foundation.[1] During the conversation, one of the panelists declared with some affirmation, "There is no question … that at some point in the future … we will have AI systems that are as smart as humans in all the domains where humans are smart." Perhaps just as memories of scenes from *The Matrix* and *The Terminator* were beginning to collectively breach the audience's imagination, he quelled the fear by adding, "Intelligence has nothing to do with the desire to dominate."

That panelist was the Turing Award winner Yann LeCun. The Turing Award is the Nobel Prize for Computing, and Yann's words were probably the most informed summarization of the nature of the threat that AI poses to our society. Yann proceeded to explain how evolutionarily speaking, if a human wasn't that smart, he needed help from others, leading to his need and consequent attempts to influence them. The threat from AI advancement, therefore, is not from the technology's autonomy but from the vested interests of humans guiding that autonomy who may want to exert control.

One may say that human distrust and competition are precisely why any form of superpower should be discouraged before it is turned into a weapon. That was as true for an atom bomb as it is for AI. But that was also true for fire if we look at it from the perspective of our distant ancestors who must have first encountered it. Yet, the only way innovation and advancement have been thwarted in human history has been by the burning of books and libraries—a mechanism that has always set the society on course for eventual demise or dictatorships.

So, can the future of generative AI catapult our society while giving us that much-desired sense of control? To understand the possibilities, let us structure our conversation around four broad areas: large-scale operational automation by integrating existing generative AI applications, improvements in the large language models underlying those applications, novel applications of generative AI enabled by ongoing innovations, and the impact of these changes on our society and economy.

Large-Scale Operational Automation

In the chapter on automations, one of the examples we discussed was how a marketing team could use generative AI to go from identifying a niche opportunity to its promotion, sale, and support. The full cycle wasn't entirely automated, though, with a number of tools involved on the way. But what if it could be, much like we saw with automated consulting in the chapter on insights? Thanks to API connections, what if all solutions could be connected to trigger each other at the right moment by receiving the required data from one solution and transmitting the required output to another?

Picking up the example of the art-and-craft organization trying to optimize customer acquisition over the holidays, let's say automated market and consumer research on third-party and first-party data reveals a new pricing opportunity for the holiday season. That triggers a web page content creation supported with imagery and articles for social media posts, which in turn not only generates short-form videos but also validates and improves them to use in optimized advertisements. Meanwhile, e-mails could be generated and sent to the right customer segment, personalized based on their available public or proprietary profiles, followed by improved offers based on their response. And in case of any recipient query, the chatbot could do the rest. All without manual intervention.

That is the operational reality that generative AI is inevitably heading toward. In some ways, it is already there because neither the above functionalities nor their integration is new. A marketer would soon be able to single-handedly plan and deploy such widespread automation in the near future. Whether she is allowed to will depend on three factors: the limits of our creativity, the technical and financial resources we can afford, and our comfort level with automation and perceived loss of control.

That last reason corresponds to many of the risks of AI that we have studied before. We discussed how generative AI could itself be used to address many of the risks. The same, unfortunately, is true for worsening them. So, as the automation capability advances, so do its risks. Robust Intelligence, for example, showed how an automation constituting a series of prompts led by its adversarial algorithms could accomplish the desired jailbreak more systematically.[2]

Improvements in Large Language Models

One of the first areas of improvement in LLM actually has nothing to do with improving the technology. It has to do with making it more globally representative of our culture and realities. That includes training LLMs on historical data and context beyond Western cultures, religions, art, and philosophies. It also implies LLMs in languages other than English. Governments and institutions across the world are launching such programs. One of the greatest LLM evolutions, then, would be to converge these and give it multilingual and multicultural diversity.

On the technological front, the concept of transformer architecture, which led to large language models (LLMs), was just one way to approach processing large volumes of data quickly. There are so many angles in which it can be improved—from yielding more relevant output to doing so in a more cost-efficient way and from requiring less data to achieve that to leveraging a completely different architectural concept. Retrieval-augmented generation (RAG), as we know, ensures the former by limiting an LLM's focus to specific documents and data fed in by a user. However, that says nothing about the LLM's ability to fetch the data from within those documents in a relevant way.

The problem here is that LLMs have a limited capacity in how much information they can process at once. Streaming LLM is an interesting solution to increase a model's contextual bandwidth as it allows the model to generalize the content it was trained on as a way to extend the context it can answer questions around.[3] Another approach is laid by the System 2 attention (S2a) concept, which regenerates the inputs (data fed in) to focus on relevant portions. To decide relevance, it leverages the LLM's ability to reason in natural language.[4]

The other problem we face with LLMs is that of rising costs. While fine-tuning LLMs can be helpful for specific use cases, they can quickly pile up for organizations, leading to high processing power requirements. Researchers at Stanford University and the University of California-Berkeley came up with S-LoRA (LoRA is low-rank adaptation, a method to use a base LLM model and fine-tune it for different use cases), which used a concept called Unified Paging. Put simply, it is like having an index in a book to guide us to the right page for the information we are looking for. S-LoRA can increase throughput four times, which allows an organization to use multiple fine-tuned models at scale.

A typical transformer architecture underlying an LLM consists of a block to deal with the attention mechanism, a mini neural network to deal with the deep learning part, residual connections to allow quick moving from one task to another, and normalization layers that ensure efficiency. So, even with scalable fine-tuning, the base LLM alone can require extensive memory and processing power. Researchers Bobby He and Thomas Hofmann proposed simplifying this structure that allows reducing the size of the underlying transformers without impacting the speed or accuracy of the model.[5] Architectural modifications do not, however, reduce the need to train and maintain big models. That is where a small language model (SLM) comes in.

SLM requires lesser data and parameters and can help reasonably enough with a variety of smaller-scale applications, which can be helpful for organizations that do not boast vast resources. One approach to accomplish this is knowledge distillation, which sees an LLM used to train a smaller model. That approach, however, can lead to an IP breach risk, as the smaller model developed by an organization would essentially take from the larger one developed by another.

A second and upcoming approach to utilizing lesser data while retaining the large model capability is liquid neural network (LNN), as attempted by the company Liquid AI. As the company's website states at the time of this writing, the concept integrates "fundamental truths across biology, physics, neuroscience, math, and computer science" to somehow build a scaled-down model that is better at "causality, interpretability, and efficiency."[6]

For a marketer, the net of it all is improvements in LLM that may make these models more accessible and usable regardless of the size of their organization.

Novel Applications of Generative AI

Earlier in the book, we discussed how real-time procuring of information that allows greater interactivity has been a gift of generative AI. But even *real time* can have many layers to it. For example, Google DeepMind's GNoME (graph networks for materials exploration) can predict the stability of new materials to significantly speed up their discovery. That doesn't make it real time but relative to the typical speed of material discovery, it's lightning fast.

It's one thing to have a system fetch answers from the Web when prompted; quite another for it to respond actively to our gestures, as we saw in the chapter on content. Such improvements in speed and efficiency can spawn novel applications across industries—from allowing two people to communicate in different languages simultaneously to allowing creators to continually edit and evolve images with simple actions. It is what makes Google's Gemini or Krea.ai so powerful.

Real-time content generation and evolution leads us to the world of mixed reality—from live multiplayer video games to producing movies. Enhanced by dynamic shape display, real-time generative AI can allow physical interactivity across great distances, as Tangible Media Group's inFORM does. Picture it like a Zoom call where one participant can control and move digital objects on the other participant's end. One could also be watching a game on screen physically rendered in real time in 3D on a table in front of it. All this gets a further boost from wearables armed with generative AI, as Solos AirGo3 has done with its smart glasses. One can expect these technologies to fundamentally change how learning and training happen, making them much more hands-on.

One cannot discount the fact that most of the novel applications of generative AI will be in conjunction with other emerging technologies, making them more powerful and capable. For example, Elon Musk's Neuralink has been testing the ability to execute computational tasks using brain waves. Soon enough, researchers at the National Institutes for Quantum Science and Technology (QST) in Japan managed to achieve 95 percent accuracy in AI-driven image generation using only brain activity.[7] This possibility can have a profound impact not only on those suffering from some form of physical paralysis but also on a perfectly fit marketer looking to generate content. It is a shot in the arm for creativity, as the physical limitations we face in translating our imagination on a computer screen start to dissipate.

Researchers have tried to take human–computer interaction a step further with the use of generative agents. Bred in immersive environments with the freedom to communicate with each other, once these agents could memorize, recall, and reflect on their past observations, they were able to interact with each other much like humans in a society would do—sharing information, forming relationships, and coordinating on plans.[8] That, of course, brings us to the threshold of artificial general intelligence (AGI).

AGI is Yann LeCun's aforementioned state of AI being as smart as humans in tasks. It is also the ultimate goal that OpenAI has been working on—a revelation that, some speculate, might have been influential during Sam Altman's much-publicized transition at the company in 2023.

Regardless of the state of AGI, AI autonomy is being actively worked upon as large-scale operational automation starts to become an organizational reality. Even the company's GPT-4 managed to power Nvidia Research's AI agent, Eureka, to successfully teach and train other robots in complex skills. This is why the possibilities with generative AI can explode in unexpected ways even in the near-term future.

Socioeconomic Shift

If we continue our march toward the realm of artificial general intelligence, GPT-5 or other more advanced GPT—whether from Open AI or another company—could imply a seismic shift on the socioeconomic landscape in several ways. First, many companies whose products rely on GPT-4 could gradually become obsolete if the more advanced versions of GPT can mimic those products on its own. Second, the impact on jobs aside, such automation can change not only how we live but also what we do for a living. Third, bad actors can misuse such capability to enormous proportions without many coming to know. What would all this mean for us?

Marketing is the practice of influencing a set of population to buy into an idea. Often, the idea leads to a monetary transaction. Take the 1986 study that claimed how advertising influenced the world by "reinforcing materialism, cynicism, irrationality, selfishness, anxiety, social competitiveness, sexual preoccupation, powerlessness and loss of self-respect"[9] as traditional values attributed to family, religion, and education took a backseat in the 20th century. In other words, marketing has always had an impact on social and economic trajectory. Sometimes it is quite obvious but at other times, it is subtle though no less impactful.

A risk specific to the marketing domain, besides the generation of fake content, is how it can strengthen the practice of subliminal marketing—initiatives aimed at influencing the audience subconsciously (i.e., without them becoming consciously aware of it). It's a largely banned practice that relies on fusing details in content that register in our minds and are then reinforced, in a fraction of a second, without us consciously noticing them. Generative AI can create such content with much more efficacy. A growing ability to read or write narratives in our brain or even our very genes holds an enormous array of possibilities that can help or harm us. The last thing we want is to make a purchase, hold an opinion or support a group and justify it, without realizing the roots of that idea.

The growing risk of AI to society and economies has seen a deluge of regulations from governments around the world, whether at a continental, national, or even provincial level. However, these regulations may create more confusion and chaos among companies if they don't align with each other. It would be difficult to build an AI product or use it in a way that meets all requirements globally. While competing countries or ones that are culturally and politically at odds may not achieve an alignment, states within a country are likely to. Sooner or later, we should see a consolidated standard in AI regulations in most locations around the world.

There is also a sense of inevitability in how generative AI may impact us psychologically. For instance, if fake content becomes so easy and commonplace in our lives, it is likely to psychologically neutralize the society to content that would have otherwise been deemed as shocking. Compromising imagery or news may become so prevalent that they come to be largely ignored as fake or humdrum. In a world plagued by fake news and reputations tattered in the blink of an eye, the ease of generating such content may compel us to not blindly believe anything and everything that we come across on social media.

To ensure that this behavior does not do injustice to the truth, mechanisms to validate generative AI content and source will likely also become commonplace. That is where this author feels that the blockchain technology will find its other footing—in maintaining a historical chain of information as an immutable source of truth, whether in upholding professional agreements or in saving a life.

Job displacement is another major risk for generative AI, but it may not be as straightforward as job losses in bulk, which many companies have traditionally executed in the face of an oncoming recession. An article in *Fortune* shared how over half of the workers tasked with market intelligence gathering were willing to prioritize a small pay cut rather than not use AI for their work.[10] It underscored the fundamental benefits of

AI in improving productivity and helping us, which has led to its rise in the first place. The onset of generative AI is a socioeconomic iteration that we have all brought to reality together. Meta's image generator Imagine, for instance, was trained on over a billion images that we publicly shared on Facebook and Instagram over the years.[11]

One could argue that former social sharing was inadvertent. Does that mean we will now limit how much we share content online? To allow public access to our content is to knowingly forego its confidentiality—the kind of trade-off we have often made to gain something else. It could be popularity, social credit, or something else. And that is okay. The important thing is to first acknowledge and accept a society's natural inclination in order to rationally understand the risks at play. Often, these risks turn out to be quite different from those imagined.

Consider generative AI's ability to generate codes and create entirely new applications—including other generative AI tools. It is natural to sound the death knell for developers until we unpack that a bit more. Say ChatGPT generates a program for an in-company app. Would that lead you as a marketer to take your developer's work away? That would first require you to learn the coding fundamentals, the full-stack tools, libraries, and steps in the app development journey to understand and make use of these AI-generated codes—something you may be unlikely to do.

Practically, generative AI's ability to generate codes is likely to be a boon for developers as it makes them more efficient and capable. Development companies, for example, would benefit from increased margins as they can now get more work done (more code generated and improved) in a fraction of time for their clients.

That said, job displacement is a real possibility with the advent of generative AI. Workers are likely to shift to newer types of roles created as a result of the shift in the operational needs of a company that can now automate a lot of what it used to need workers for. The shift is likely to be among the frontline workers, middle managers, and executives alike, though to varying degrees and with varying time delays between job loss and job creation. In such a scenario, there is likely to be a further push for concepts like universal basic income, job displacement calculators, and open disclosures in the estimated and actual socioeconomic impact of an organization's adoption of generative AI.

To enable the protection of our interests against the risks and to reliably propel the economy with generative AI, expect a deluge of governance positions announced by countries, communities, and corporations alike. As the hype around generative AI settles down and users get a better sense of its usage, possibilities, and fallouts, governments and organizations are bound to establish principles and regulations to better manage and control the technology. The European Union, for instance, reached a consensus on a penalty-driven protection mechanism around the responsible use of generative AI.

Similar to privacy laws like GDPR, generative AI regulations are likely to directly impact marketing teams in terms of both the data they hold and its treatment. Unlike the former regulations, these will also extend to how teams execute initiatives. For example, while privacy laws only concerned themselves with whether an individual's data was protected and treated as per their consent, generative AI laws would also have to ensure that the system is not used to generate illegal or dangerous content from scratch, whether or not it used any existing data. These laws would also look to prevent organizations from gaining unfair advantages, pursuing anticompetitive practices, or leveraging generative AI in ways that are harmful to its stakeholders and the society alike.

Dessert

The unstoppable nature of research and innovation in AI has rendered frequent improvements in the technology inevitable. If it has played a role in lowering costs and enabling scale with greater automation, it is likely to do that even better in the future. We saw in this chapter how new products and services take birth as generative AI matures, and how both organizations and people are likely to respond as a culture and society. By now, it must be clear how marketers sit at the junction of a technological and socioeconomic evolution, given how the initiatives they take can impact the organization, its jobs, and entire societies. In the next chapter, we will summarize everything we have covered so far to conclude our learning journey around generative AI for marketing.

CHAPTER 12

Summary

As I attempt to pen this summary, a dilemma beckons: Should I simply upload each chapter on ChatGPT and prompt it to summarize them for me? The passion and joy of writing for an author aside, wouldn't this exercise be much quicker? The tool will receive clarity on the tonality and focus points desired. A quality check will follow. We could even have the tool summarize each chapter in the unique style of a different author—Tolkien would discuss the evolutionary journey of marketing in Part 1, Hemmingway would discuss the philosophy of AI in Part 2, and J.K. Rowling would share the magic that different generative AI tools have made possible in Part 3. The end product will likely be amusing and informative—the perfect mix. The real question, though, is: How would you as the reader feel about it?

There is no perfect answer to this question because extremes aside, we are yet to decide on what's OK and what's not with generative AI. A lot of what we decide to feel is based on the speculative degree of risks with using the technology in a given situation—risks that could range from another party's victimization to a general sense of unfairness. For a user not accountable for the nature of her ChatGPT exploration on either of those accounts though, many of these impeding walls fall away. What remains is a personal benefit at a low cost (direct or collateral in nature)—a powerful incentive to use generative AI. In such a scenario, once we begin, our continued use of this technology becomes inevitable. That is the law of inertia that governs us all. That is also why Victor Hugo famously said, "No power on Earth can stop an idea whose time has come."

We have covered a long journey in this book to envision revenue growth in the generative AI era. The purpose of this book was as much to enable the organizational application of the different strategies and initiatives as to ensure that they were done in a responsible way. We traced the evolutionary steps of both marketing and generative AI for that precise reason before exploring how the two can work together. Let us bring forth the key highlights we touched upon along the way.

Part 1

We began Part 1 of this book by taking stock of the changing landscape of marketing. The first chapter discussed how the function took birth under the changing supply-demand equation as organizations first felt the need to differentiate themselves from the competition to lure customers and capture a market they were now sharing with an increasing number of players. We saw why brand resonance became important but remained elusive for most companies until generative AI opened up certain subjective possibilities.

As we flew past the prewar and postwar decades to arrive at the present time, we saw how marketing became tremendously specialized to generate silos, and how boundaries to a marketer's knowledge made AI's value difficult to realize. The chapter also deliberated on the other ongoing organizational shifts. This included the external factors coming in from shareholder expectations, supply chain constraints, and changing consumer behaviors. The internal forces, meanwhile, included productivity issues, skill gaps, cost pressures, and changing structural dynamics.

The second chapter narrowed our focus on marketing in the new organization reality discussed above. It began by briefly revisiting the various elements of the marketing domain, bringing into focus the interplay of insights and brand identity, and legal and ethical considerations, that are crucial to generative AI enablement. We also learnt from industry examples why the current structure comes in the way of efficient and effective execution for revenue growth, particularly limiting AI's usability.

The chapter then proposed a new marketing structure of functions built on the three core components of AI use cases—content, automation, and insights—feeding the required resources dynamically into project areas that carried clear and distinct marketing objectives. It briefly elaborated on these three core components that would coexist with the fourth one—frontline workforce and contracted third parties.

Keeping in mind the changing workforce and market dynamics, the new structure had twofold motivation. On one hand, it enabled the cross-functional and planned adoption, data and process alignment, and operational execution that AI needs. On the other hand, it introduced much-needed agility for an organization to quickly adapt to changing market demands and internal realities by reallocating resources, resetting objectives, and most importantly, ensuring that all stakeholders were reliably and continually informed on the marketing initiatives and insights. This in turn would help avoid redundancies, stack fatigue, clashing priorities, and delays in realizing returns on the marketing investments made.

Part 2

Part 2 was about understanding AI—the technology, its value, its journey from the mathematical simplicity of statistics to its humanlike capability today, and the journey that organizations must follow in leveraging it successfully and responsibly.

We went over the nature of AI and its fundamental concept of pattern recognition to understand what makes it important and a necessity in organizations looking to survive or sustain competitive advantage today. We also pondered over the fears of AI taking over—a recurring theme that must be addressed every time. We then followed the chain of needs that have led to innovations in AI. Patterns were recognizable with traditional statistical techniques as well, but only with known variables. To uncover hidden patterns that were being driven by unknown variables, needed machine learning.

That path opened a Pandora's box as more advanced problems emerged. We responded with advanced solutions that could allow systems to learn from mistakes or understand natural language communication. The natural next step was to increase the ability of pattern recognition to the level required for more advanced tasks, like recognizing images or predicting schizophrenia. The answer lay in mimicking how our brains work with neural networks. That was deep learning.

Deep learning required a lot of data and a lot of processing power, making it out of reach of many. Generative AI was born with a new kind of model architecture which could address the issue of speed and time, in particular. It fused the aforementioned techniques to give us the interactive supertools that made practical AI finally accessible by all and formed the genesis of this book.

The fourth and fifth chapters of this book attended to AI journeys. We discussed AI readiness assessments and the topics it can be taken up on. The TUSCANE approach focused on data in particular, as required by an AI system. The vision, systems in use, and the accountabilities to maintain good data are all important. The next decision to make was whether to build or buy an AI solution for the chosen use case if AI was the best approach at all. We used a FAB approach to find pre-existing solutions to take stock of the requirements and our readiness levels to use AI, answer whether AI was the best investment to make, and build a proof of concept to quickly qualify that option, if at all feasible and affordable in our organization.

It was at this juncture that we began looking at the risks AI brings, a topic we'd return to later in the book. The common risks with AI were related to system incompatibility and interference, job losses, crippling dependencies, data accessibility, security, legal liability, and model performance. These risks mandated robust policy formulation. From an ethical point of view, that meant putting approval, reporting, and accountability criteria in place, in addition to ensuring clear communication and training of employees. From the perspective of operational efficiency, the chapter drew parallels with human relationships to ensure AI tools were treated ethically, responsibly, and optimally. It also ensured sobriety and expectation management in getting value out of these tools sustainably.

We learnt that the deployment of AI journeys involves failing quickly to course correct, which in turn requires a project champion and a team of early adopters to try and qualify the solution first. It also involves finalizing the relevant key performance indicators (KPIs) that will best reflect not only the AI model's performance but also that of its users and, consequently, that of the business. These metrics could measure the scalability and robustness of the solution in addition to its accuracy in different circumstances that may otherwise pass under the radar and prove costly. They would also look at improvements in productivity, revenue growth, and/or cost reduction as a result of the AI deployment. It is important to keep a 360-degree perspective to also consider AI's collateral impact on factors like the organization's brand as an employer or vendor.

Part 3

Ready to discuss the fusion of marketing and generative AI, we began this part with a reflection on how the technology has impacted the domain. We recalled the content, automation, and insights functional groups to walk through an example of project areas they would collaborate on. These areas—temporary or permanent—would focus on distinct objectives of marketing, be it product strategy, brand building, sales or customer support, for instance. We also discussed how frontline workers fit into this puzzle to maintain organizational agility without collateral damage on one's job. That in turn led us to discuss the job displacement fears and to see it in the context of the multidimensional benefits and risks that generative AI opens us to

Some risks can be specific to generative AI, such as those of AI hallucination or jailbreak prompts. While we discussed business and resource planning with generative AI, we also covered how to manage the risks that come with the technology. That included policy making, training users, supporting governments and communities, and even using generative AI itself for corrective and preventative measures.

The most prevalent use of generative AI so far has been prompt dependent. Prompting can ensure the relevance and accuracy of the response we get from these solutions. To achieve that, we discussed a range of factors we must clarify for a tool like ChatGPT to help it grasp the context around our question, the role to step into, the nature of the task, and the conditions it must adhere to while executing it. Persona, voice, style, parameters, channel, output type, topic, goal, action, reference material, and other conditionalities were listed as some of the recurring components of effective prompts. With the right prompting, a user could learn topics quickly, solve problems, create content, increase their productivity, and gather insights that may otherwise be elusive.

The next three chapters looked at the three functional groups of content, automation, and insights. Starting with content, we mapped the varying levels of maturity an organization may have and what a truly content-mature one looks like. We also gained a deeper understanding of the different types of content that can be generated with generative AI— text, images, videos, sounds, hybrid files, codes, and entire entities like an AI influencer for social media. The use cases of all this content could be applied to range from content plans to product and user experience and from promotional and support content to marketing optimization, as in the case of real-time (or predictive) identification of the best-performing advertising copy.

Automation appeared as a major area of generative AI application that is likely to eclipse even content generation in terms of value and prevalence in organizations. That is because it can offer teams the opportunity to significantly lower costs, optimize or enhance resources, expand the skillset, and gain a competitive advantage. At the same time, these elements can also help qualify the need for—or the feasibility of—taking up an automation initiative.

The sustainability of using an automation successfully over time, its impact on other existing or future technologies within an organization, and the overwhelming or impeding effect it can have on the workforce were some of the other considerations to make. We also dove deeper into the specific nature of tasks that can make it automation-friendly. These included how rule-based and predictable the task was and whether it required intuition, sentiment, or critical decision making to mandate human control.

This ninth chapter also covered the three main automation techniques: directly using pre-existing generative AI applications, connecting to existing models or tools, and building a proprietary generative AI application or LLM. The chapter concluded with examples showcasing how a team could use widespread automation to accomplish a series of tasks around identifying and launching a new offering and seeing it through to revenue realization. The integration of such automation could enable a one-person army of operational execution.

As we turned our attention to insights generation, we learnt its omnipresence in anything generative AI does. These insights could be used for strategy and planning; preparing a persuasive business case to highlight the scope, investment, and benefits involved with the plan; efficiently executing it; tracking the ongoing status to validate our initial estimations; and ensuring agility to course correct as and when needed.

Success with insights banked on two considerations. One was on proper measurement, where we explored how generative AI is helping companies pivot to a deeper understanding of its customers than was possible, without privacy invasion. The other consideration was contextuality, where techniques like retrieval-augmented generation (RAG) could help users get answers specific to their realities and proprietary data.

Part 4

The final part of this book is where we now stand. Before we began our summary, this part allowed us to step back and ponder over what comes next. There's so much that goes beyond predictability when it comes to generative AI innovation and the society it may create. We revisited our discussion on the technology's impact on humans in this chapter and stratified this deliberation on the future across four areas: operational automation with existing applications, improvements in their models, newer use cases, and the socioeconomic impact.

We discovered several areas of ongoing research that are looking to equip LLM architecture to require less data, become more efficient, and increase its relevance and overall capability. We also ventured into generative AI's real-time enablement of mixed reality and the plethora of applications that come with it. We discussed wearables, using the technology with just our brain waves, and even a case of AI agents socializing among themselves.

The final deliberation was on the social and economic front, warranting increasing regulations worldwide as the dust around generative AI settles down. Calculators estimating the impact on jobs may become a part of necessary disclosures in organizations looking to adopt generative AI. The regulations, though, may not cover the psychological shift this technology brings in us, changing our perspective on topics ranging from taboo to fake news. The chapter also briefly toyed with the idea of using blockchain to keep an immutable record of truth and enabling a universal basic income that a generative AI world may mandate for financial security, especially while jobs go through the transition phase of deletion and creation.

Generative AI opened the door to memory and reflection by AI, which now allows AI agents to communicate, socialize, and plan their day in what is one of the closest milestones to artificial general intelligence—a human-level capability that many institutions are trying to achieve in AI. As Yann LeCun stated, there is an inevitability to it, but to picture a dystopian era induced by AI autonomy is to misinterpret what drives domination. Given a human history laden with examples of rulers who tried to subdue the society, our information and knowledge are key to ensure that the AI era follows the examples of rulers who instead made the society prosperous.

So, to bring our discussion full circle, it is for you to decide how you'd feel if ChatGPT had written this chapter after all. There are no right answers, for they are often contextual and fluid. But your judgment—ideally one brainstormed over—may help establish your appetite for, acceptance of, and adherence to the generative AI usage in your organization. That is important because, having read this book, you are now equipped to begin a personal journey to lead or influence the technology's future and influence how both your organization and your society can benefit from it.

Stay happy. Stay productive!

Notes

Chapter 1

1. Nelson-Field and Erica (2010).
2. Robert (1992).
3. Liang (2024).

Chapter 2

1. Upadhyay (2021).
2. Coulson, Mauser, Holloway, Lazer, and Gross (1980).
3. Kulova (2021).
4. Caye, Hemerling, Lovich, Humblot-Ferrero, Potier, and Werner (2022).
5. Kulova (2021).
6. Walsh and Nitin (2023).
7. Nelson and Ollen (2023).

Chapter 4

1. Wharnsby (2023).
2. Grossman (2010).
3. Upadhyay (2020).
4. Cai (2023).
5. Upadhyay (2020).

Chapter 5

1. Sathe and Ruloff (2023).
2. Upadhyay (2020).
3. Ibid.
4. Ibid.

Chapter 6

1. Verhoef, Broekhuizen, Bart, Bhattacharya, Dong, Fabian, and Haenlein (2019).
2. Storbacka and Moser (2020).
3. Kaput (2023).
4. McKensie (2023).
5. Davis (2023).
6. Pixeltie (2023).
7. OpenAI (2023).
8. McKinnon (2023).
9. Vasquez (2023).

Chapter 7

1. Prompt ROI (2023).
2. Open AI (2023).

Chapter 8

1. MaxAI (2023).
2. Hanson Robotics (2023).
3. Bhaimiya (2023).
4. Hawkins (2023).
5. Yang (2023).
6. The Museum of Modern Art (2023).

Chapter 9

1. Walmart (2023).
2. Browne (2023).
3. Open AI (2023).
4. Parr (2023).
5. Cook (2023).

Chapter 10

1. Neurons (2023).
2. Nelson and Ollen (2023).
3. The Mars Agency (2023).

Chapter 11

1. World Science Festival (2023).
2. Knight (2023).
3. Xiao, Tian, Chen, Han, and Lewis (2023).
4. Weston and Sukhbaatar (2023).
5. He and Hofmann (2023).
6. Liquid Team (2023).
7. Matsumoto (2023).
8. Park, O'Brien, Cai, Morris, Liang, and Bernstein (2023).
9. Pollay (1986), pp. 18–36.
10. Daniel (2023).
11. Edwards (2023).

References

"AI: Grappling With a New Kind of Intelligence." 2023. World Science Festival. www.worldsciencefestival.com/programs/ai-grappling-with-a-new-kind-of-intelligence/ (accessed December 15, 2023).

"Being Sophia." 2023. Hanson Robotics. www.hansonrobotics.com/being-sophia/ (accessed December 15, 2023).

"Liquid AI: A New Generation of AI Models from First Principles." 2023. Liquid Team Liquid. www.liquid.ai/blog/new-generation-of-ai-models-from-first-principles (accessed December 15, 2023).

"Predict." 2023. Neurons. www.neuronsinc.com/predict (accessed December 15, 2023).

"Prompt Engineering." 2023. Open AI. https://platform.openai.com/docs/guides/prompt-engineering/strategy-test-changes-systematically (accessed January 2, 2024).

"Shoptalk 2023: New Tools for Old Tricks." 2023. The Mars Agency. www.themarsagency.com/post/shoptalk-2023-new-tools-for-old-tricks/ (accessed December 15, 2023).

"Text to Shop." 2023. Walmart. https://texttoshop.walmart.com/ (accessed December 15, 2023).

"VCGPT." 2023. Open AI. https://chat.openai.com/g/g-Nldd8JwN4-vcgpt (accessed December 15, 2023).

Bhaimiya, S. 2023. *An Agency Created an AI Model Who Earns Up to $11,000 a Month Because It Was Tired of Influencers 'Who Have Egos'*. Business Insider. www.businessinsider.com/ai-influencer-aitana-clueless-agency-tech-spain-2023-11 (accessed December 15, 2023).

Browne, R. 2023. "An AI Just Negotiated a Contract for the First Time Ever—and No Human Was Involved." CNBC. www.cnbc.com/2023/11/07/ai-negotiates-legal-contract-without-humans-involved-for-first-time.html (accessed December 15, 2023).

Cai, K. 2023. "From OpenAI to Stripe, Artificial Intelligence Is Remaking The Cloud." Forbes. www.forbes.com/sites/kenrickcai/2023/08/08/artificial-intelligence-remaking-the-cloud/ (accessed December 15, 2023).

Caye, J.M., J. Hemerling, D. Lovich, M. Humblot-Ferrero, F. Potier, and R. Werner. 2022. "Why the World Needs Generative Leaders." BCG. www.bcg.com/publications/2022/all-about-generative-leadership-and-its-benefits (accessed January 1, 2024).

Cook, J. 2023. "5 ChatGPT Prompts to Secure Brand-Boosting Press Coverage." Forbes. www.forbes.com/sites/jodiecook/2023/11/21/5-chatgpt-prompts-to-secure-brand-boosting-press-coverage/ (accessed December 15, 2023).

Coulson, J.M., F. Ferdinand, R.J. Holloway, W. Lazer, and I. Gross. 1980. "Marketing Issues." *Journal of Marketing.* www.jstor.org/stable/1251236 (accessed February 16, 2024).

Daniel, W. 2023. "AI Is So Indispensable to This Profession That 41% of the Workers Who Use It Say They'd Rather Take a Pay Cut Than Go Without the Technology." Fortune. https://fortune.com/2023/12/06/generative-ai-at-work-pay-cut-rather-than-lose-tools/ (accessed December 15, 2023).

Edwards, B. 2023. "Meta's New AI Image Generator Was Trained on 1.1 Billion Instagram and Facebook Photos." ArsTechnica. https://arstechnica.com/information-technology/2023/12/metas-new-ai-image-generator-was-trained-on-1-1-billion-instagram-and-facebook-photos/ (accessed December 15, 2023).

Grossman, L. 2010. "November 10, 1999. "Metric Math Mistake Muffed Mars Meteorology Mission." Wired. www.wired.com/2010/11/1110mars-climate-observer-report/ (accessed December 15, 2023).

Hawkins, A. 2023. "How Chinese Influencers Use AI Digital Clones of Themselves to Pump Out Content." The Guardian. www.theguardian.com/world/2023/nov/06/chinese-influencers-using-ai-digital-clones-of-themselves-to-pump-out-content (accessed December 15, 2023).

He, B. and T. Hofmann. 2023. "Simplifying Transformer Blocks." *Arxiv.* https://arxiv.org/abs/2311.01906 (accessed December 15, 2023).

Kaput, M. 2023. The 2023 State of Marketing AI Report. Marketing Artificial Intelligence Institute. www.marketingaiinstitute.com/blog/2023-state-of-marketing-ai-report (accessed December 15, 2023).

Knight, W. 2023. "A New Trick Uses AI to Jailbreak AI Models—Including GPT-4." Wired. www.wired.com/story/automated-ai-attack-gpt-4/ (accessed December 15, 2023).

Kulova, I. 2021. "Change Management as a Marketing Opportunity." *International Scientific Journal "Science. Business. Society."* https://stumejournals.com/journals/sbs/2021/1/5.full.pdf (accessed February 16, 2024).

Kulova, I. 2021. "Change Management as a Marketing Opportunity." *International Scientific Journal "Science. Business. Society."* https://stumejournals.com/journals/sbs/2021/1/5.full.pdf (accessed February 16, 2024).

Liang, A. 2024. "AI to Hit 40% of Jobs and Worsen Inequality, IMF Says." BBC. www.bbc.com/news/business-67977967 (accessed January 16, 2024).

Madori-Davis, D. 2023. "Tech Spark AI Raises $1.4 Million to Create ChatGPT Alternative." TechCrunch. https://techcrunch.com/2023/11/15/tech-spark-ai-closes-1-4-million-to-create-chatgpt-alternative/ (accessed December 15, 2023).

Matsumoto, K. 2023. "AI-Generated Imaging Using Brain Activity Hits Record 75% Accuracy: Japan Research." The Mainichi. https://mainichi.jp/english/articles/2023_201/p2a/00m/0sc/018000c (accessed December 15, 2023).

MaxAI. 2023. "The Outworld." Youtube. www.youtube.com/watch?v=s1AXcc Dlm6A (accessed December 15, 2023).

McKensie, L. 2023. "Edtech Companies Jump on Generative AI Bandwagon." Edscoop. https://edscoop.com/edtech-companies-generative-ai/ (accessed December 15, 2023).

McKinnon, J.D. 2023. "Biden Taps Emergency Powers to Assert Oversight of AI Systems." *The Wall Street Journal*. www.wsj.com/politics/policy/biden-to-use-emergency-powers-to-mitigate-ai-risks-cf7735d5?mod=djem10point (accessed December 15, 2023).

Nelson, Ken and Ollen, Kathleen. 2023. "How Organizations Can Expand Their Marketing Measurement Capabilities," The Wall Street Journal. https://deloitte.wsj.com/cmo/how-organizations-can-expand-their-marketing-measurement-capabilities-01674835025, (December 15, 2023).

Nelson, K. and O. Kathleen. 2023. "Loss of Customer and Media Data Warrants a New Approach to Measurement." *The Wall Street Journal*. https://deloitte.wsj.com/cmo/loss-of-customer-and-media-data-warrants-a-new-approach-to-measurement-01669917192 (accessed December 15, 2023).

Nelson-Field, K. and E. Riebe. 2010. "The Impact of Media Fragmentation on Audience Targeting: An Empirical Generalisation Approach." *Journal of Marketing Communications*. www.tandfonline.com/doi/abs/10.1080/135272 66.2010.484573 (accessed February 16, 2024).

OpenAI. 2023. "GPT-4 Technical Report." OpenAI. https://cdn.openai.com/papers/gpt-4.pdf (accessed December 15, 2023).

Park, J.S., J. O Brien, C.J. Cai, M.R. Morris, P. Liang, and M.S. Bernstein. 2023. "Generative Agents: Interactive Simulacra of Human Behavior." *Arxiv*. https://arxiv.org/abs/2304.03442 (accessed December 15, 2023).

Parr, B. 2023. Linkedin. www.linkedin.com/posts/benparr_introducing-vcgpt-a-gpt-that-i-trained-activity-7129930293251088385-0gX6/ (accessed December 15, 2023).

Pixeltie. 2023. "The Evolution of visual expression." Youtube. www.youtube.com/watch?v=wXQGZUU70Aw (accessed December 15, 2023).

Pollay, R.W. 1986. "The Distorted Mirror: Reflections on the Unintended Consequences of Advertising." *Journal of Marketing* 50, no. 2, pp. 18–36. www.researchgate.net/publication/233894821_The_Distorted_Mirror_Reflections_on_the_Unintended_Consequences_of_Advertising (accessed February 16, 2024).

Prompt ROI. n.d. https://app.promptroi.io/ (accessed December 15, 2023).

Robert, M. 1992. "Market Fragmentation versus Market Segmentation." *Journal of Business Strategy*. www.emerald.com/insight/content/doi/10.1108/eb0395 17/full/html, (accessed February 16, 2024).

Sathe, M. and K. Ruloff. 2023. "The EU AI Act: What It Means for Your Business." EY. www.ey.com/en_ch/forensic-integrity-services/the-eu-ai-act-what-it-means-for-your-business (accessed December 15, 2023).

Storbacka, K. and T. Moser. 2020. "The Changing Role of Marketing: Transformed Propositions, Processes and Partnerships." *National Library of Medicine*. www.ncbi.nlm.nih.gov/pmc/articles/PMC7587521/ (accessed February 16, 2024).

The Museum of Modern Art. 2023. "Documentation of Unsupervised—Machine Hallucinations—MoMA." *Youtube*. www.youtube.com/watch?v=H9wr2hx1PY0/ (accessed December 15, 2023).

Upadhyay, M.A. 2020. *Artificial Intelligence for Managers: Leverage the Power of AI to Transform Organizations & Reshape Your Career*. BPB Publications.

Ibid.

Ibid.

Ibid.

Ibid.

Upadhyay, M.A. 2021. *Modern Marketing Using AI: Leverage AI-enabled Marketing Automation and Insights to Drive Customer Journeys and Maximize Your Brand Equity*. BPB Publications.

Vasquez, K. 2023. "New Tool Detects AI-Generated Chemistry Papers." C&en. https://cen.acs.org/policy/publishing/New-tool-detects-AI-generated/101/i38 (accessed December 15, 2023).

Verhoef, P.C., T. Broekhuizen, Y. Bart, A. Bhattacharya, J.Q. Dong, N. Fabian, and M. Haenlein. 2019. "Digital Transformation: A Multidisciplinary Reflection and Research Agenda." *Journal of Business Research*. www.sciencedirect.com/science/article/pii/S0148296319305478 (accessed February 17, 2024).

Walsh, M. and N. Mittal. 2023. "To Scale GenAI, Companies Need to Focus on 3 Factors." *Harvard Business Review*. https://hbr.org/2023/12/to-scale-genai-companies-need-to-focus-on-3-factors (accessed January 1, 2024).

Weston, J. and S. Sukhbaatar. 2023. "System 2 Attention (Is Something You Might Need Too)." *Arxiv*. https://arxiv.org/abs/2311.11829v1 (accessed December 15, 2023).

Wharnsby, T. 2023. "Blue Jays GM Atkins Says Manager Schneider Made Decision to Pull Berrios From Game 2." CBC Sports. www.cbc.ca/sports/baseball/mlb/blue-jays-ross-atkins-end-of-season-1.6990255 (accessed December 15, 2023).

Xiao, G., Y. Tian, B. Chen, S. Han, and M. Lewis. 2023. "Efficient Streaming Language Models With Attention Sinks." *Arxiv*. https://arxiv.org/abs/2309.17453 (accessed December 15, 2023).

Yang, Z. 2023. "Deepfakes of Chinese Influencers Are Livestreaming 24/7." MIT Technology Review. www.technologyreview.com/2023/09/19/1079832/chinese-ecommerce-deepfakes-livestream-influencers-ai/ (accessed December 15, 2023).

About the Author

Malay A. Upadhyay has been one of the early authors in the field of AI Management. He devised some of the first managerial frameworks over the course of his roles as a COO with SalesChoice (an award-winning AI platform-as-a-service), Masterclass Instructor with the U.S. Artificial Intelligence Institute, and Author of the AI Management series of books. Few of the prestigious accolades he has earned on the way include being profiled as one of the Most Influential Business Leaders to Watch by *CEO Time Magazine* and acknowledged as one of the Top 10 Pioneering Business Leaders by *Mirror Review*.

Malay's educational courses reflect his knack for devising innovative solutions to organizational challenges and his expertise in AI-led growth enablement. They seamlessly distill the complexities of AI and organizational growth into best practices that are characterized by their lucidity and practical viability. These can be explored in USAII's Certified AI Transformation Leader program as well as popular platforms such as Udemy, Reed Learning, Quench, and Michael Management.

Having trained leaders across many fields and industries globally, Malay has also lent his expertise as an adviser in organizations and academia. He played a crucial role in the launch of the AI Directory and was part of the European AI Alliance for the formulation of the European Commission's AI policy.

Malay's strength lies in his ability to stitch macroeconomic trends with the ground realities of businesses. He was awarded Excellence at Bocconi University (Milan) for his prediction on the insurgence of a new form of currency. The novelty of his viewpoints combined with creative delivery make for a compelling guide on not only the realities facing professionals today but also the ones they are likely to encounter tomorrow.

Malay holds an MBA from Queen's University (Canada), an MSc in Marketing Management from Bocconi University (Italy), and a Bachelor of Engineering from Manipal University (India).

Sources: LinkedIn: www.linkedin.com/in/malayaupadhyay
Amazon author page: www.author.com/author/malayaupadhyay

Index

OTHER TITLES IN THE MARKETING COLLECTION

Naresh Malhotra, Georgia Tech, Editor

- *Proximity Marketing* by Rajagopal
- *Winning With Strategic Marketing* by David Altounian and Mike Cronin
- *Brand Positioning With Power* by Robert S. Gordon
- *Multicultural Marketing Is Your Story* by Eliane Karsaklian
- *Marketing of Consumer Financial Products* by Ritu Srivastava
- *The Big Miss* by Zhecho Dobrev
- *Digital Brand Romance* by Anna Harrison
- *Brand Vision* by James Everhart
- *Brand Naming* by Rob Meyerson
- *Fast Fulfillment* by Sanchoy Das
- *Multiply Your Business Value Through Brand & AI* by Rajan Narayan
- *Branding & AI* by Chahat Aggarwal
- *The Business Design Cube* by Rajagopal
- *Customer Relationship Management* by Michael Pearce

Concise and Applied Business Books

The Collection listed above is one of 30 business subject collections that Business Expert Press has grown to make BEP a premiere publisher of print and digital books. Our concise and applied books are for...

- Professionals and Practitioners
- Faculty who adopt our books for courses
- Librarians who know that BEP's Digital Libraries are a unique way to offer students ebooks to download, not restricted with any digital rights management
- Executive Training Course Leaders
- Business Seminar Organizers

Business Expert Press books are for anyone who needs to dig deeper on business ideas, goals, and solutions to everyday problems. Whether one print book, one ebook, or buying a digital library of 110 ebooks, we remain the affordable and smart way to be business smart. For more information, please visit www.businessexpertpress.com, or contact sales@businessexpertpress.com.